DIY Comic Book; Do It Yourself Comic Book

ISBN-13: 978-1-937981-67-9

Author: Kambiz Mostofizadeh

Publisher: Mikazuki Publishing House

TIPS ON STORYTELLING

a) Use linear storytelling. Start with an introduction of the protagonist (the good guy) and the antagonist (the bad guy) as this is the first step in the story. Then include stories that will work up to the problem, which is the 2nd step in the story. Then create stories that will present the resolution of the problem, which is the 3rd step. This is the basic three act story consisting of introduction, problem, and resolution. Use this model as it is time-tested and is proven as being effective for linear storytelling.

b) Use fewer words to convey more. Do not use extra dialogue or extra storytelling that is not related to the introduction, problem, and/or resolution. Any scene in the story and/or any dialogue in the story should be a means to convey the introduction, problem, or resolution. Anything unrelated or extra should not be included in the story.

c) Think of your protagonist and your antagonist and know what their qualities are. The antagonist or bad guy you create should be as powerful as or more powerful than the protagonist so as to keep the story interesting. Your protagonist's and antagonist's qualities should be listed and used as a point of reference when creating dialogue. The good guy does not have to be typical and can be an anti-hero if you choose. The point is that the qualities should be what differentiate your protagonist and antagonist and lead to their failures or successes.

d) Base your story around the protagonist or good guy. The conflict with the antagonist (bad guy) is what defines your story.

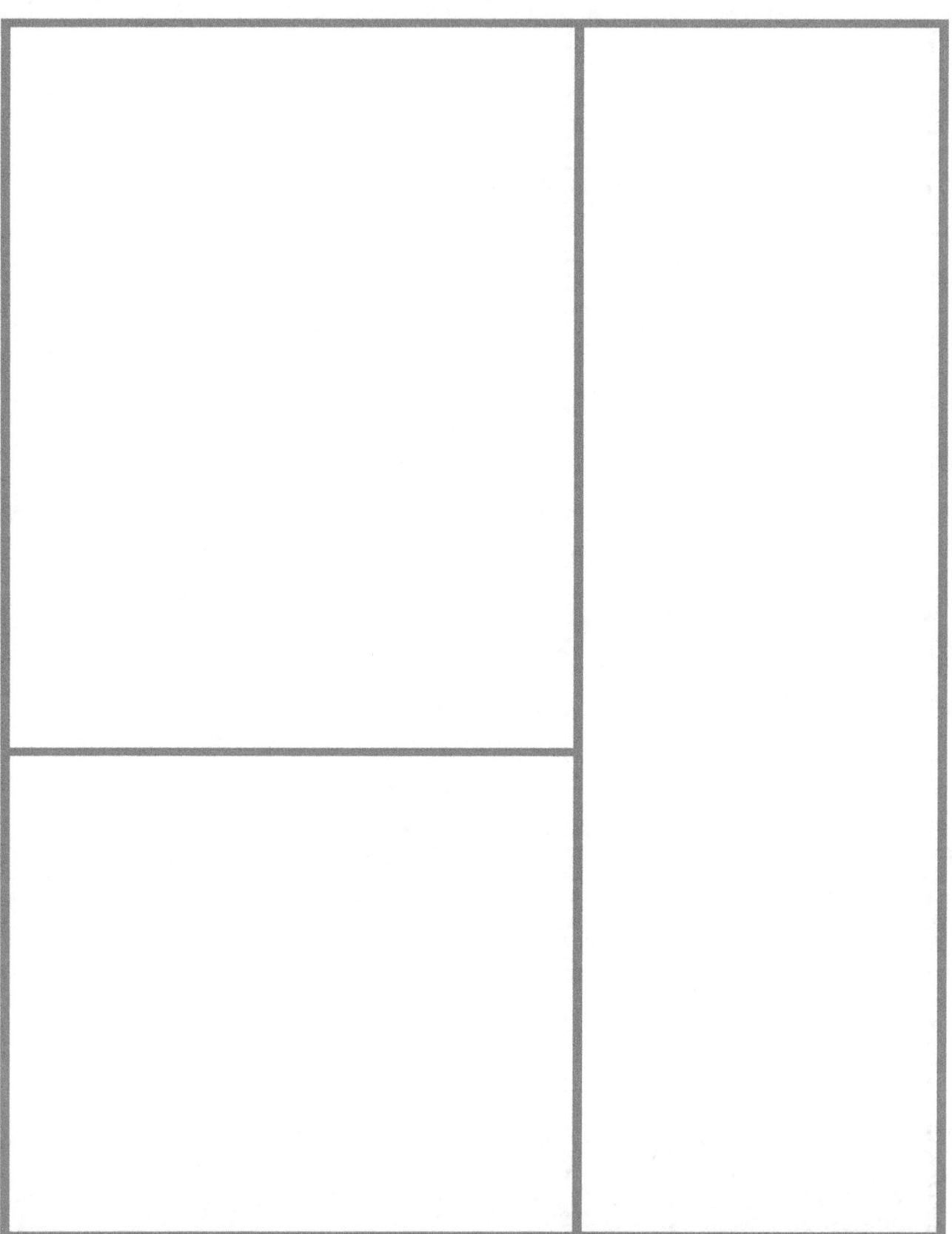

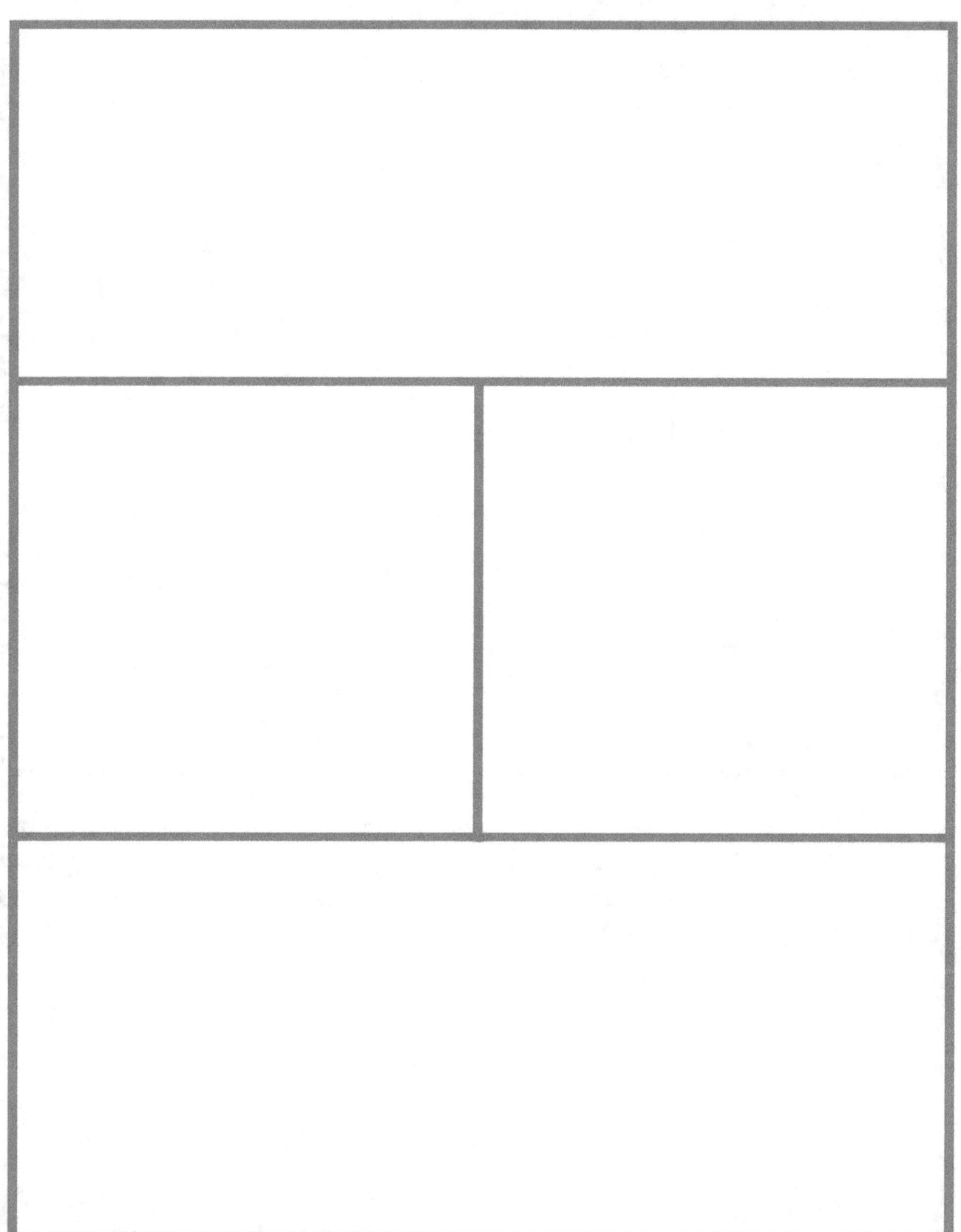

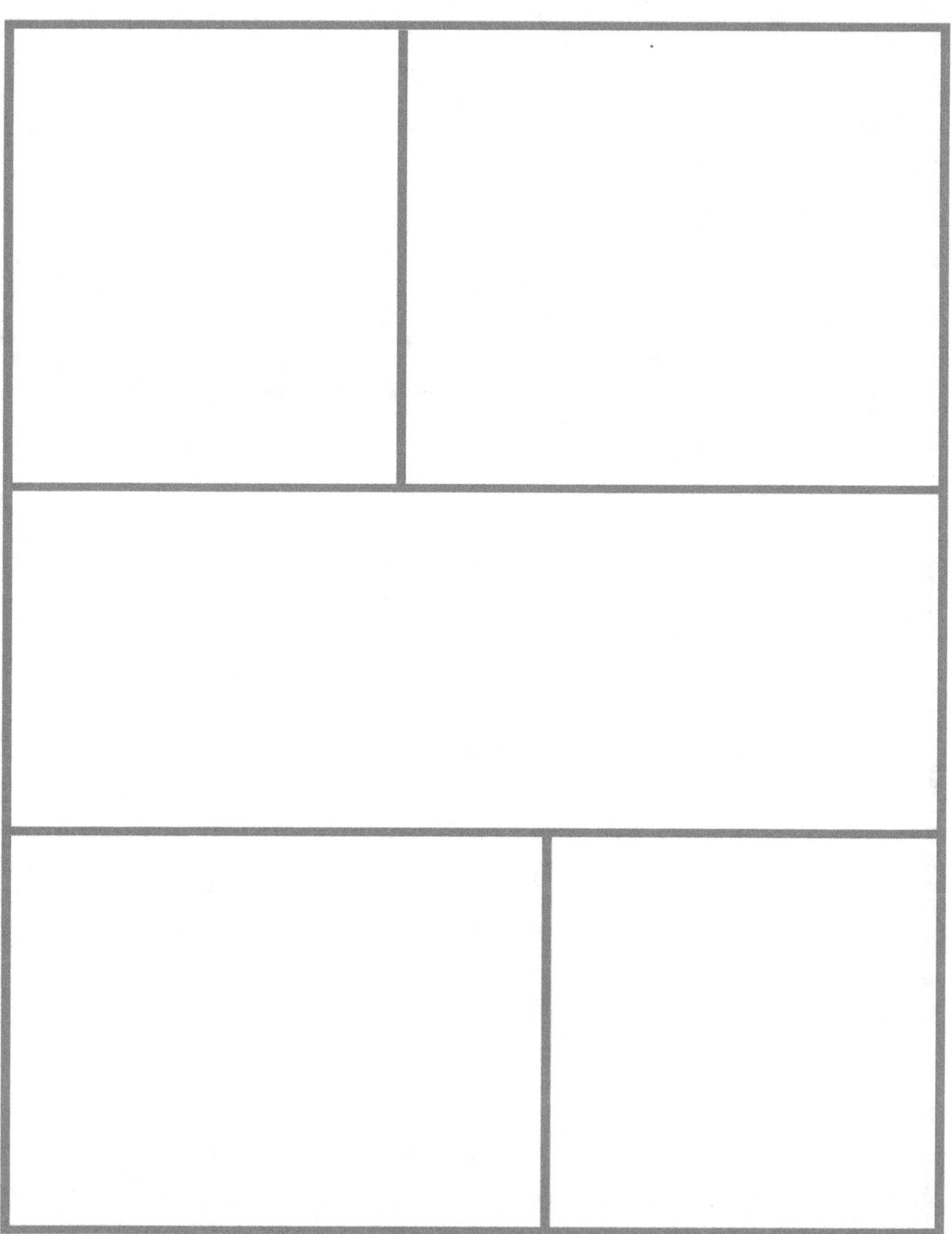

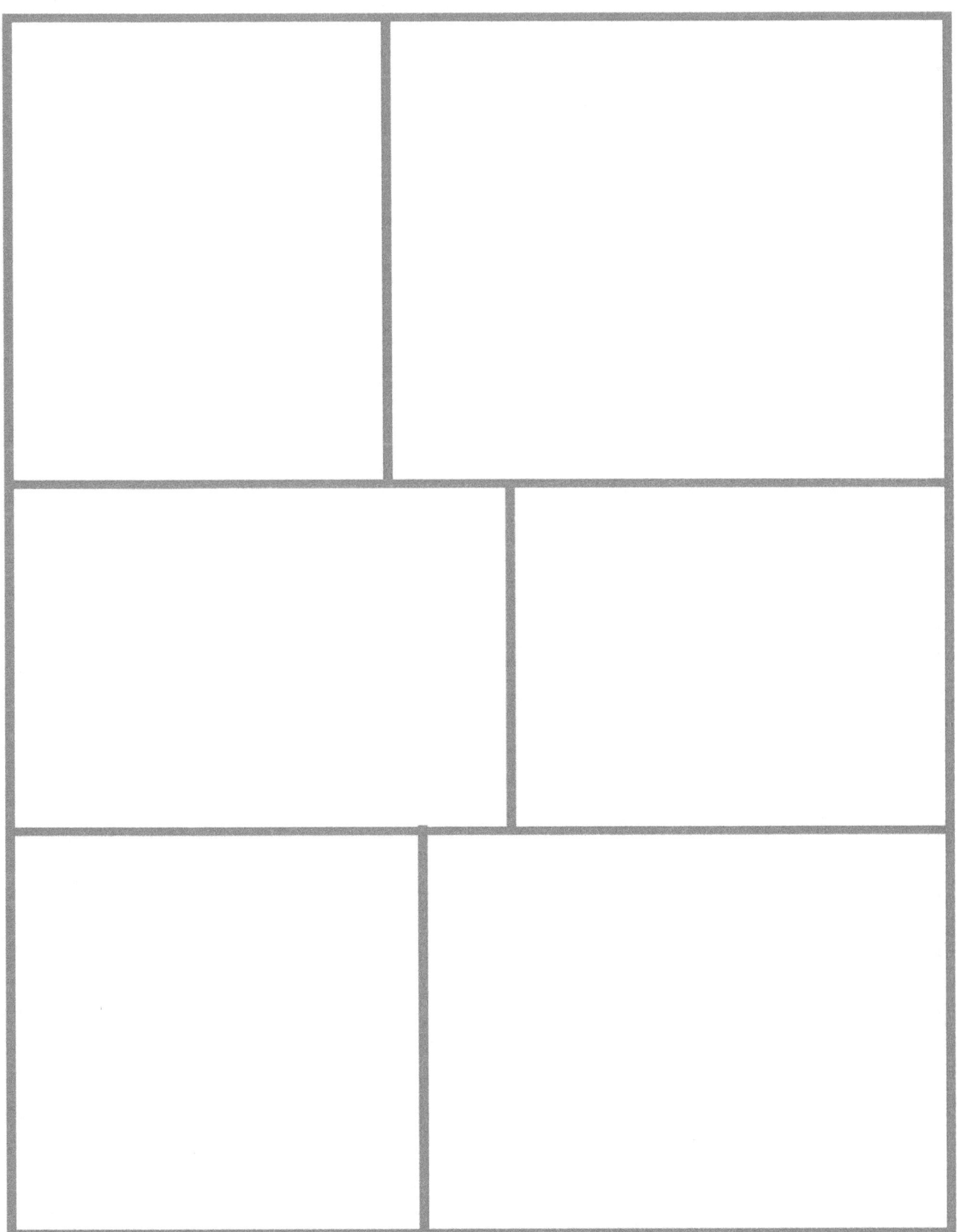

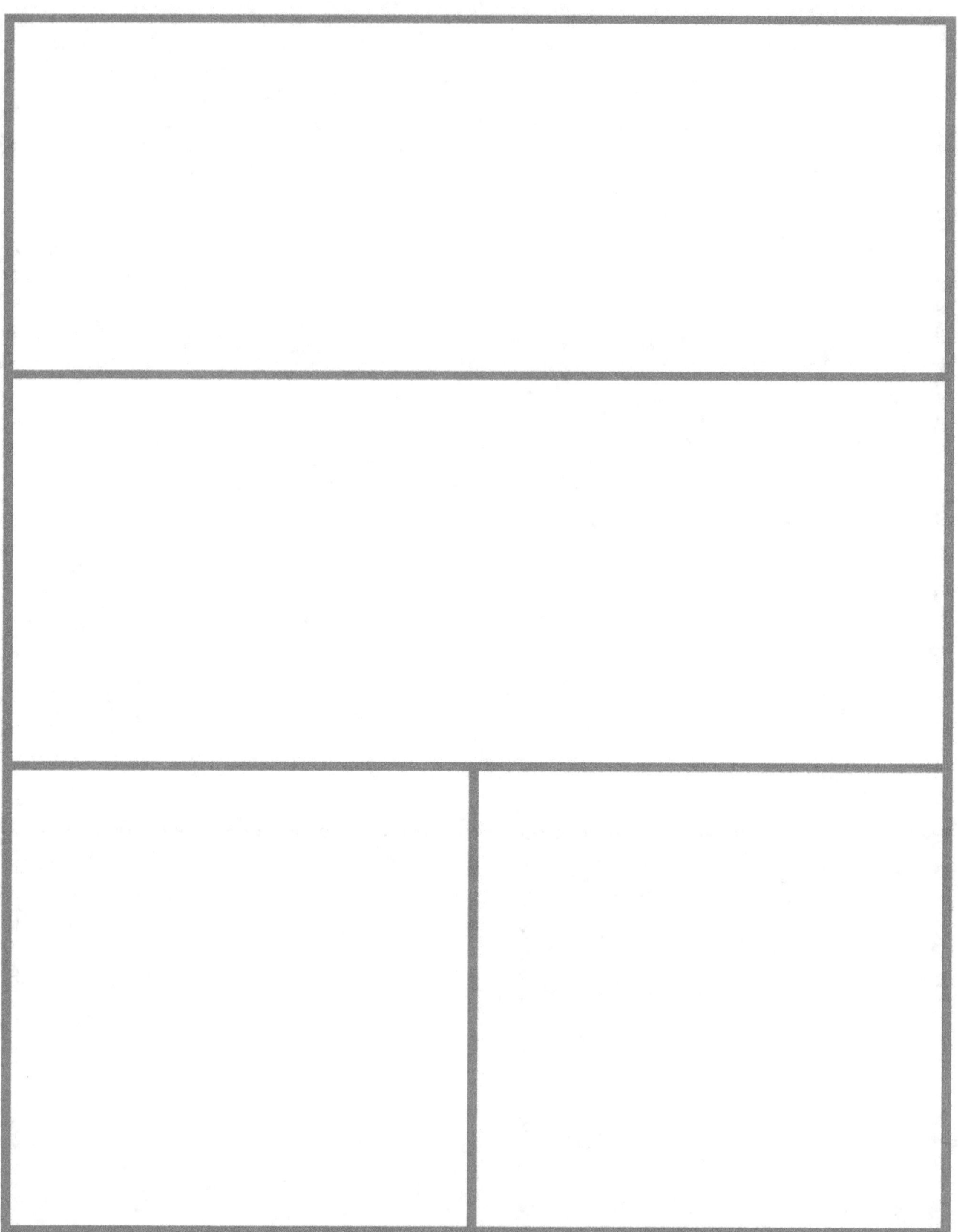

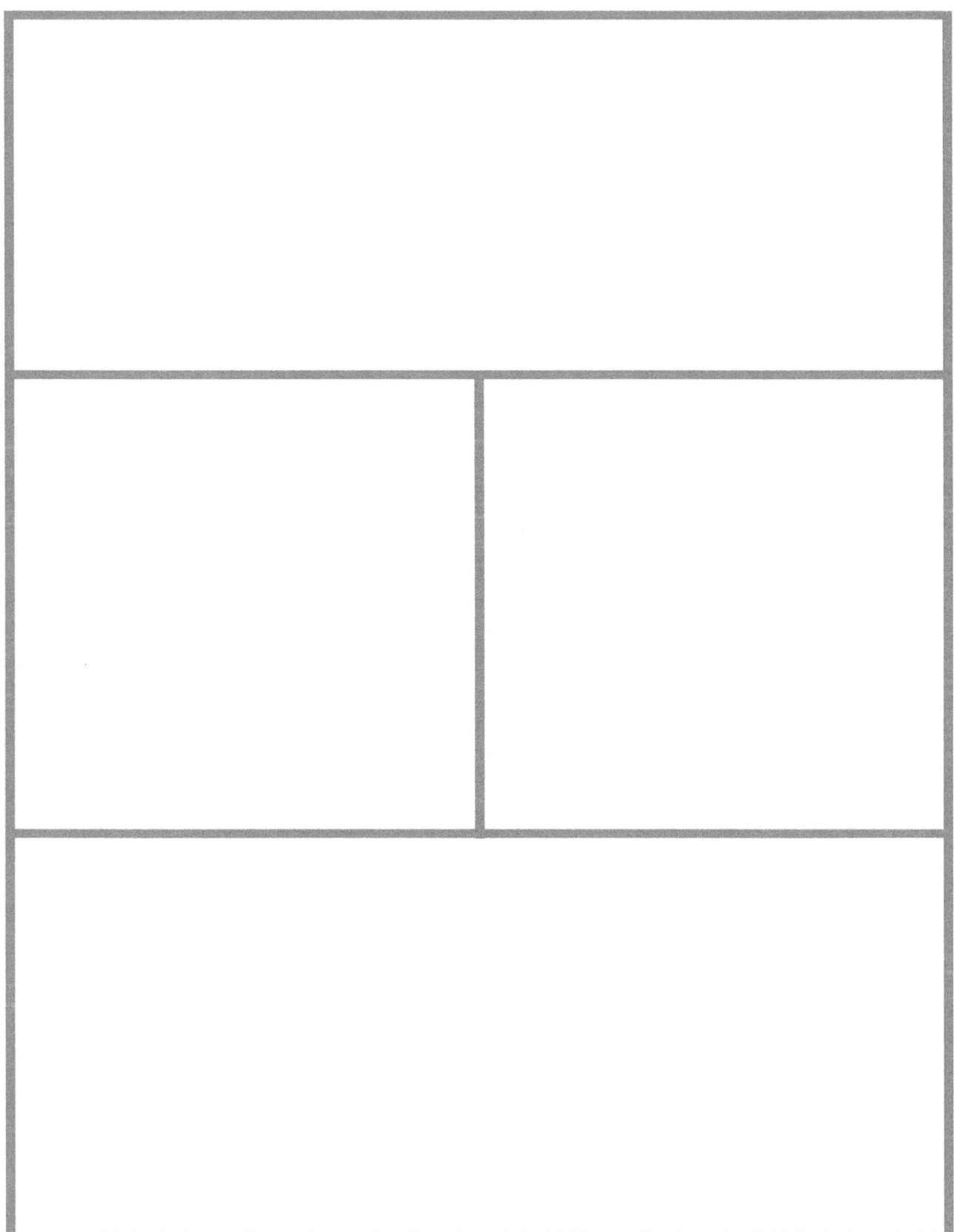

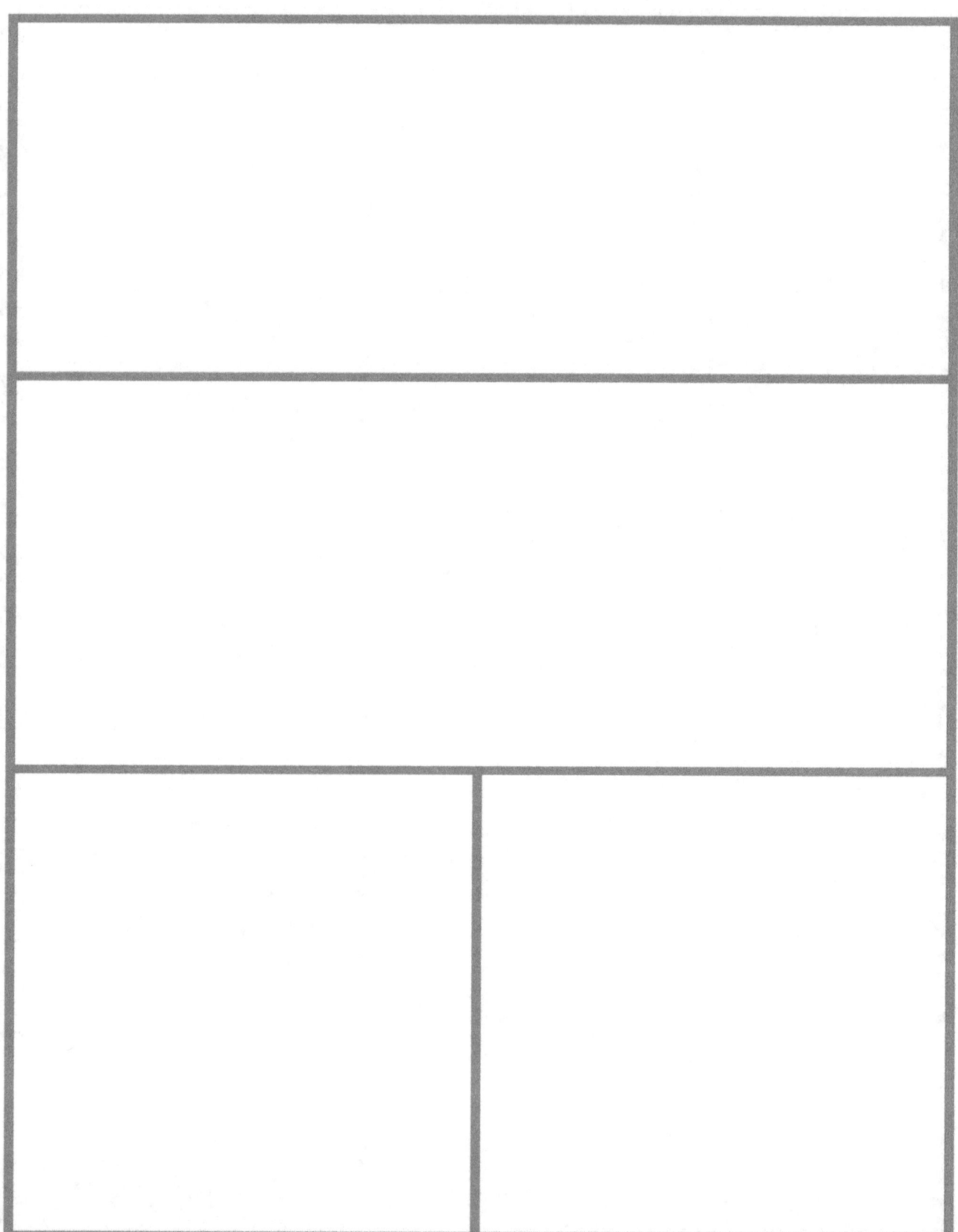

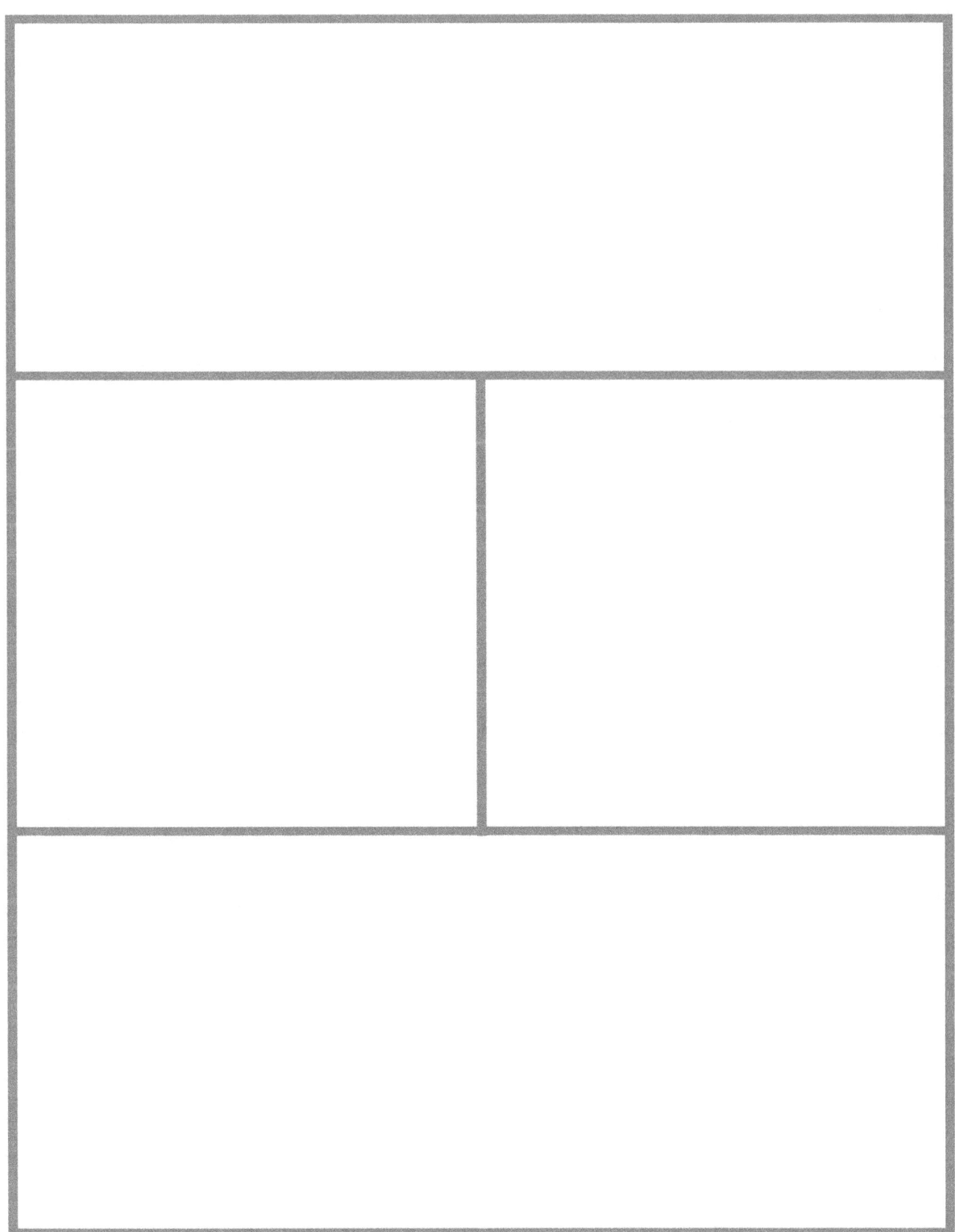

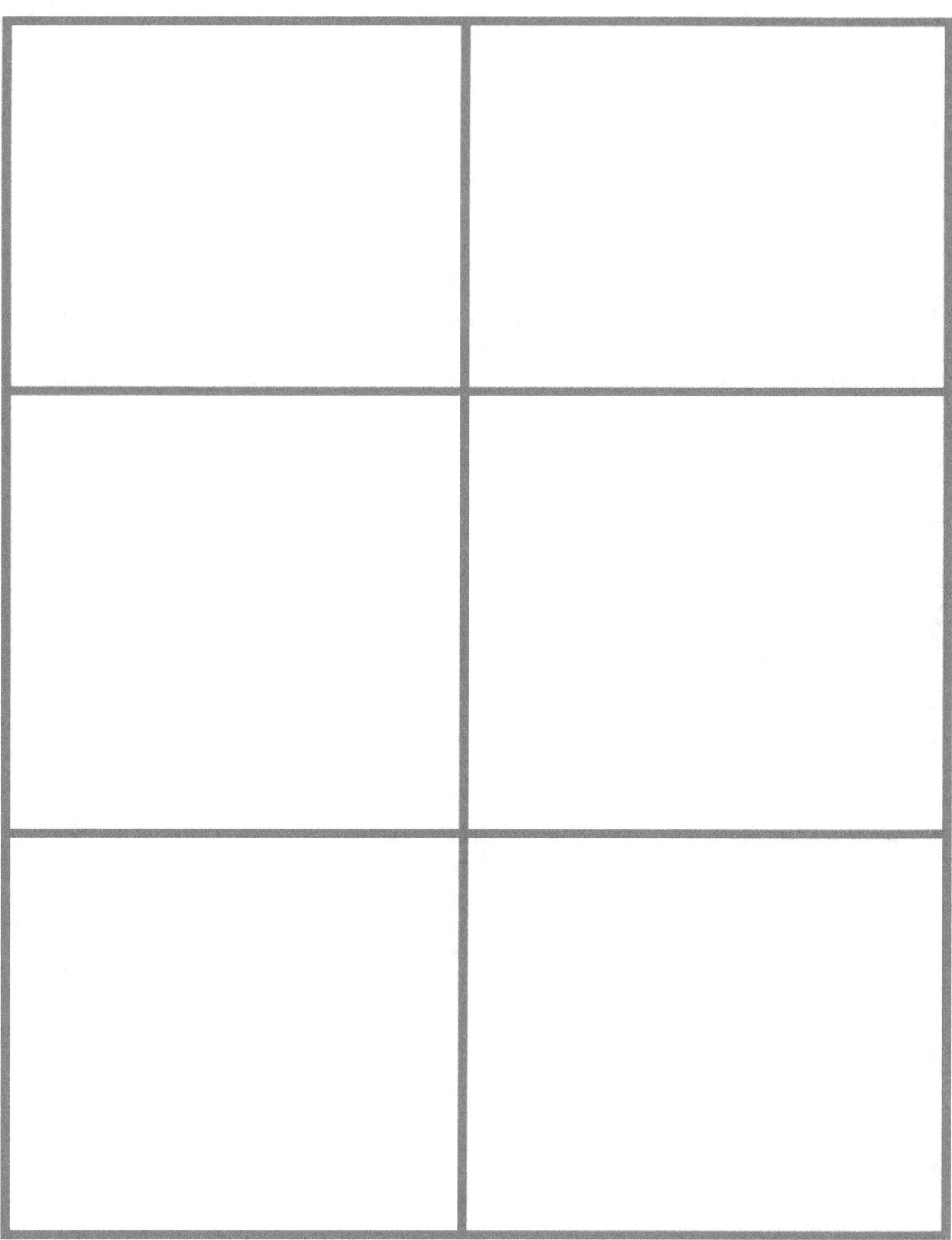

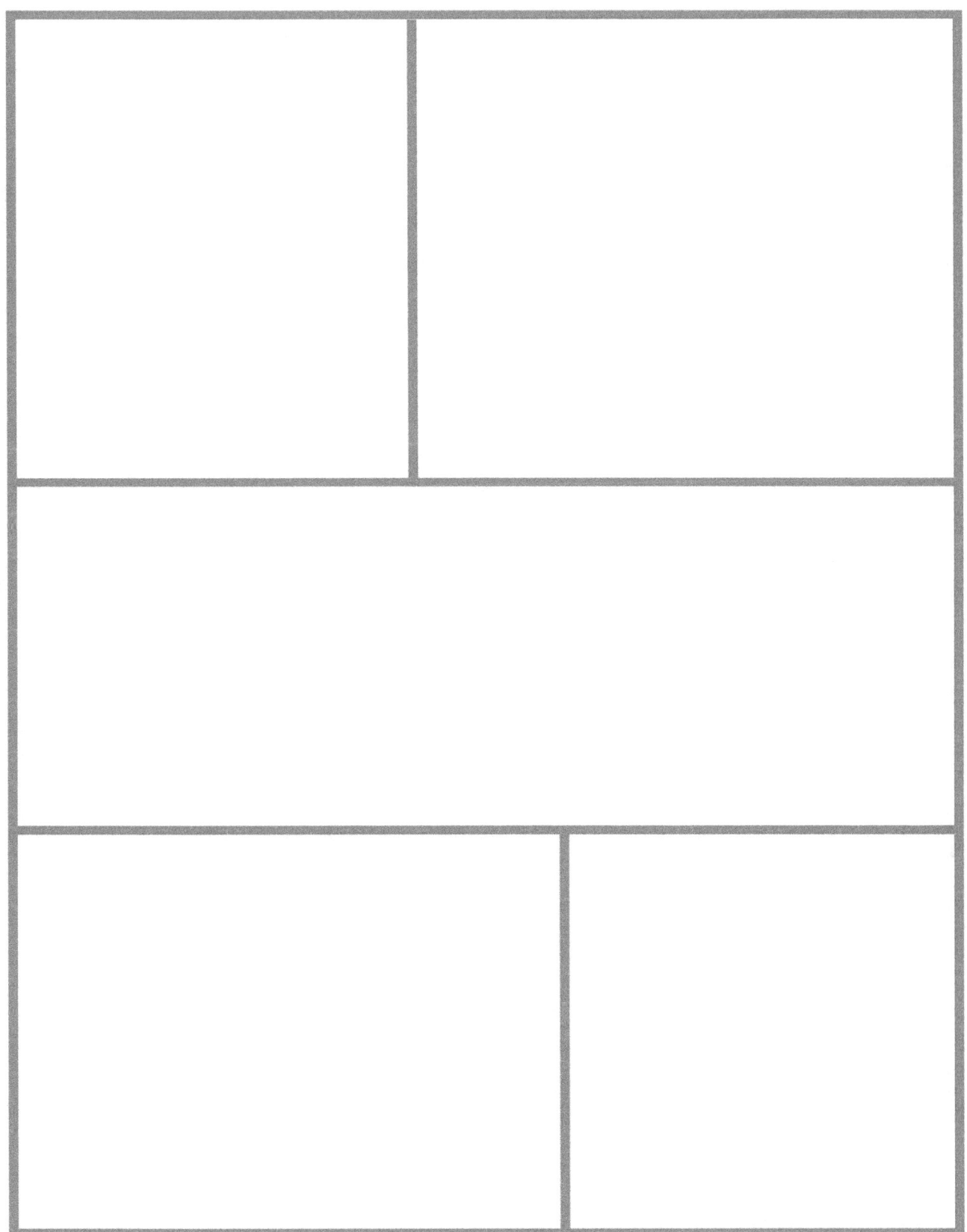

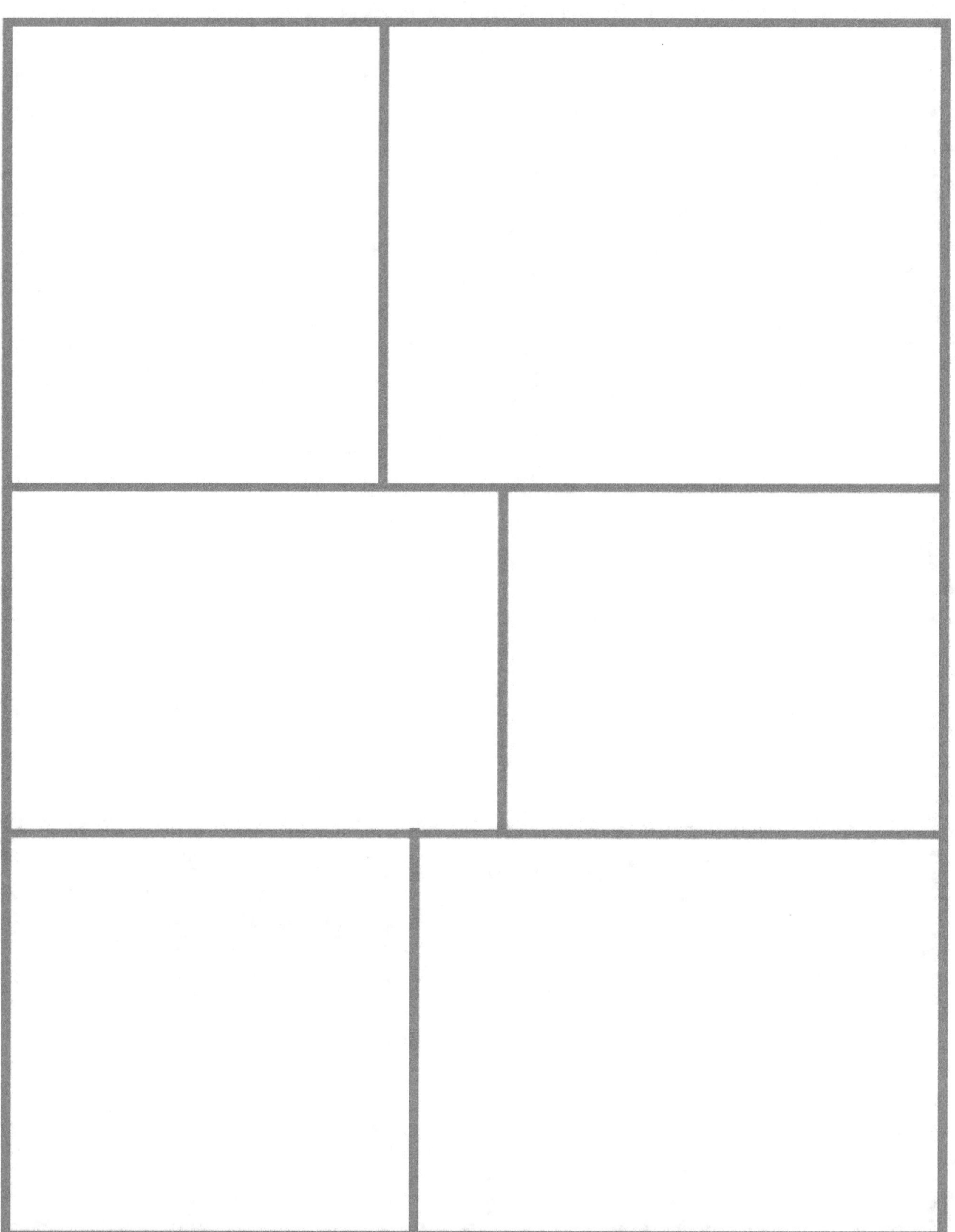

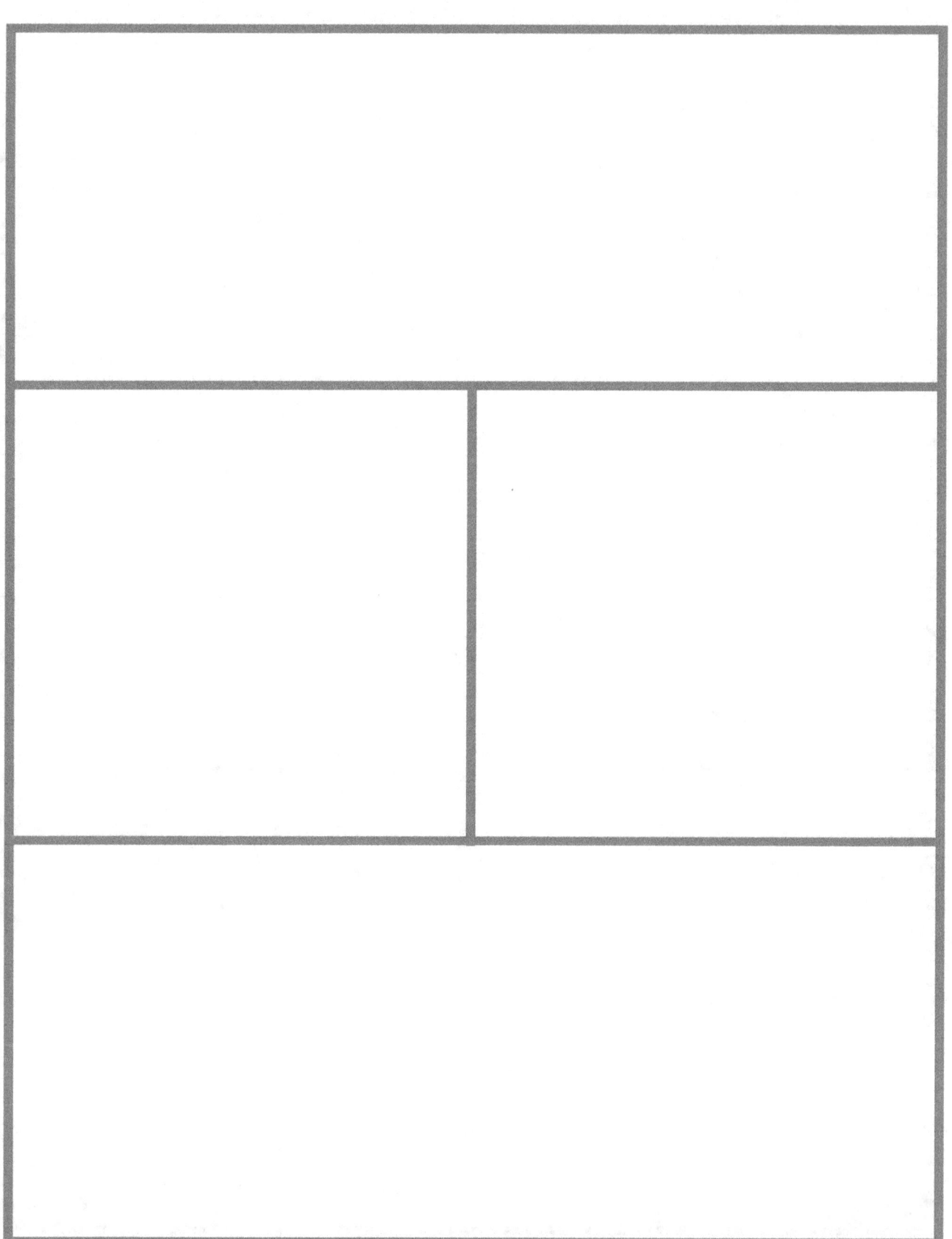

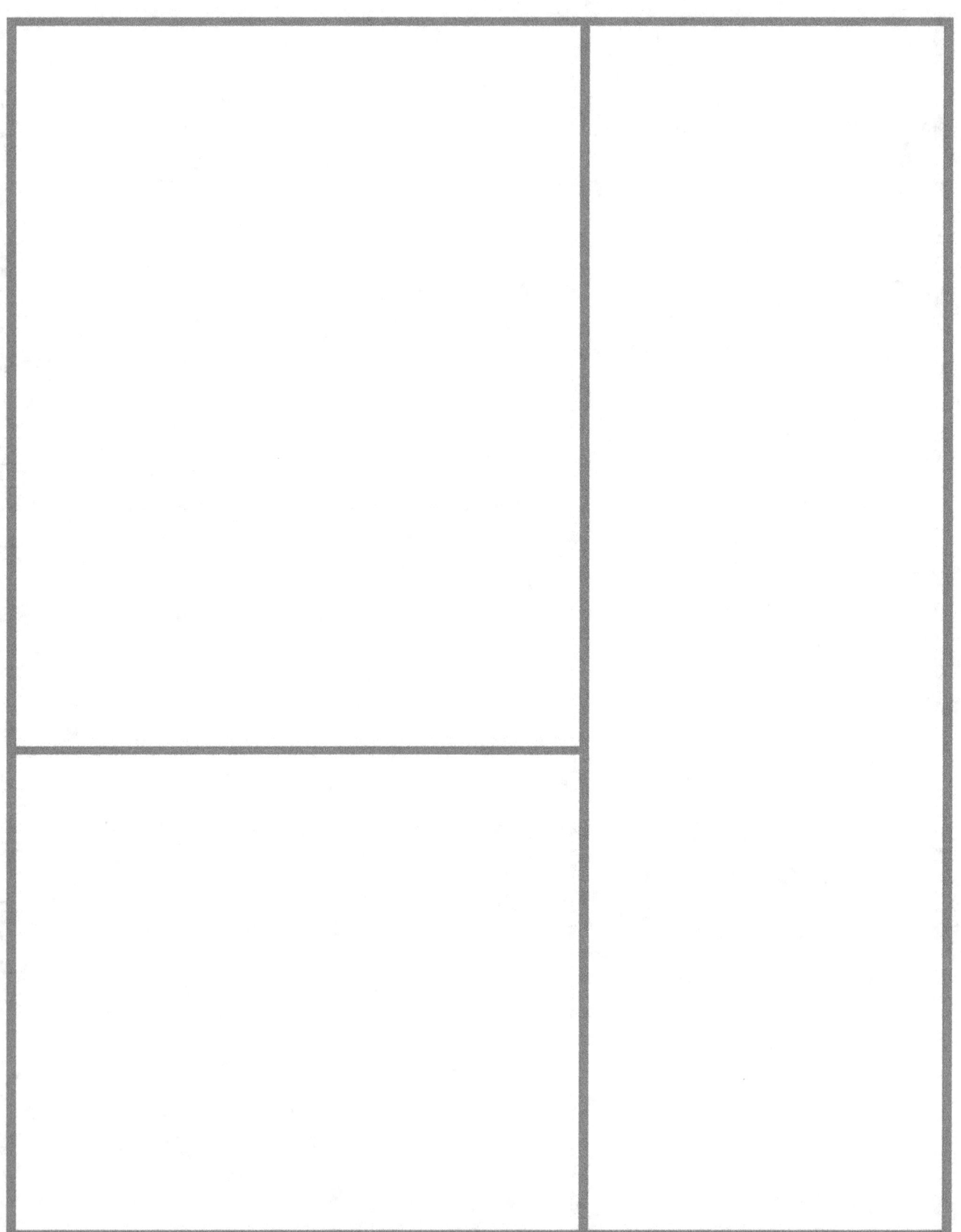

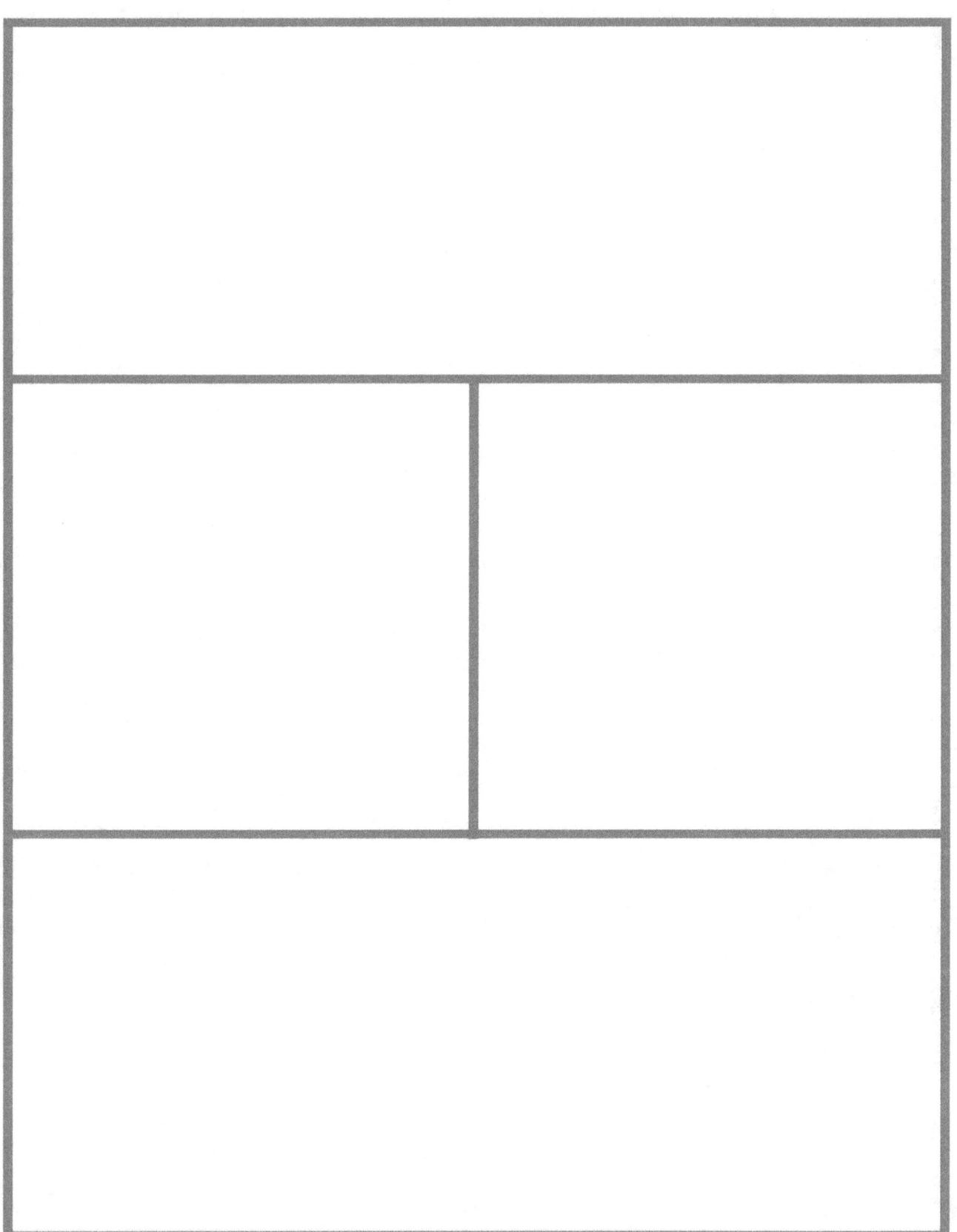

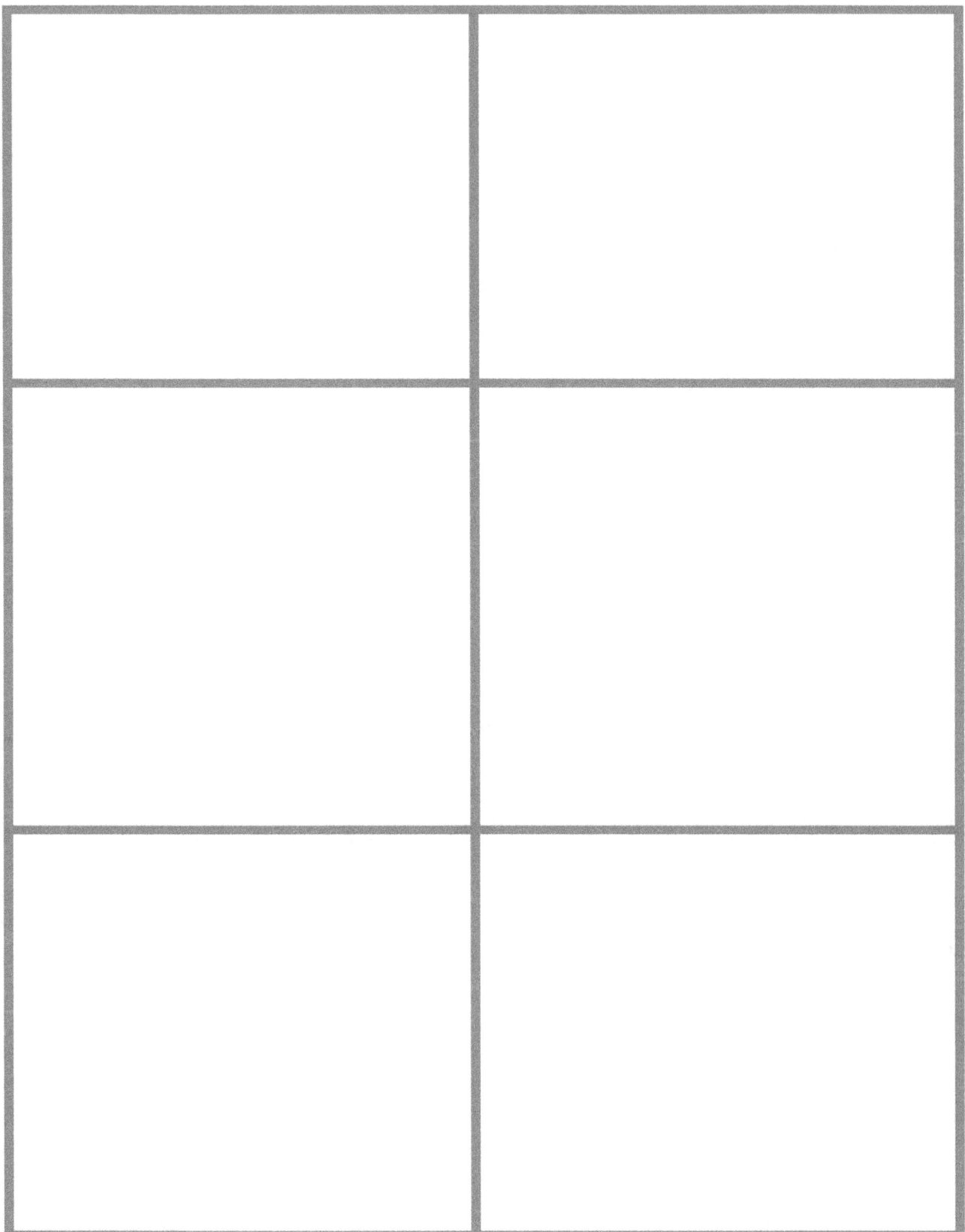

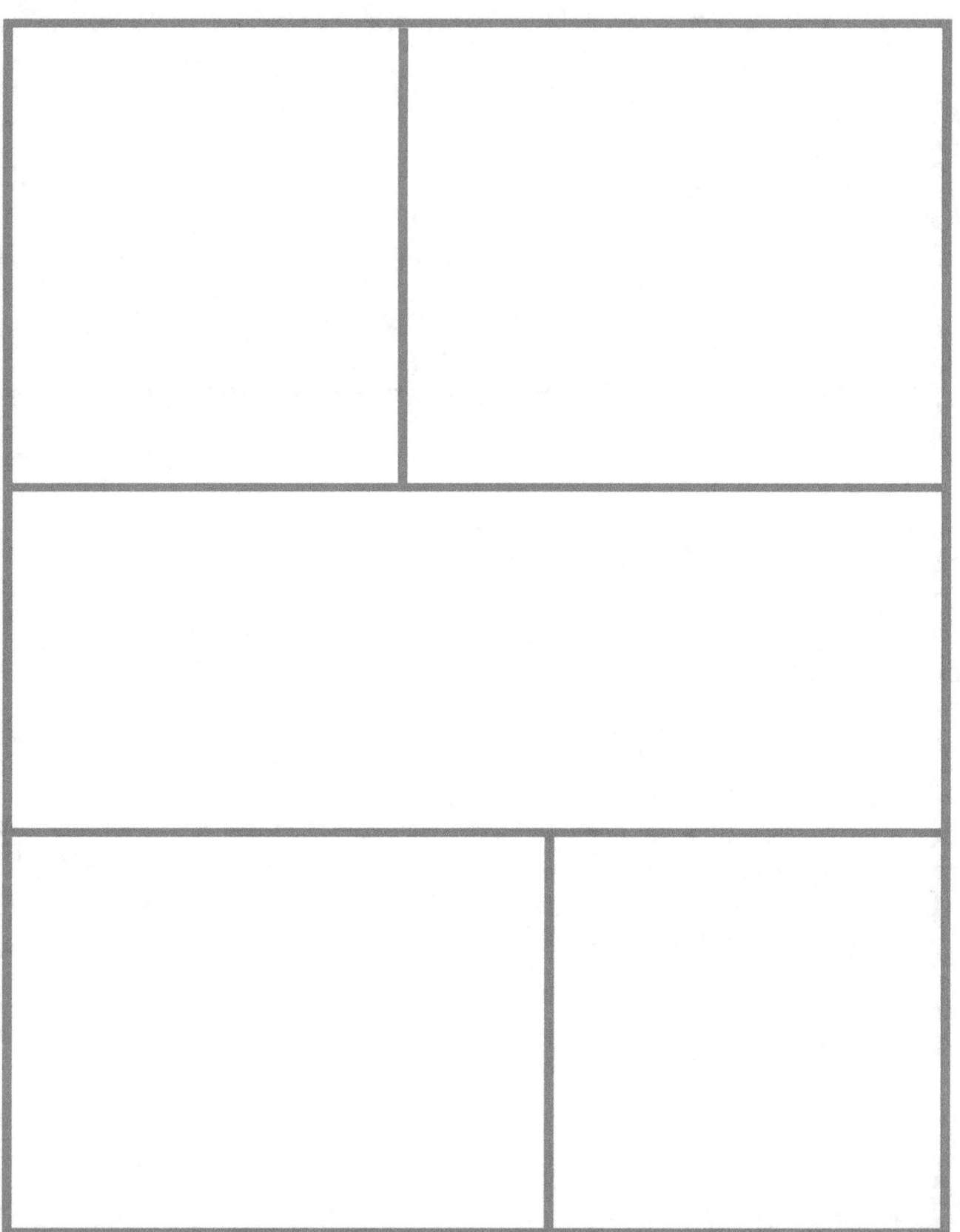

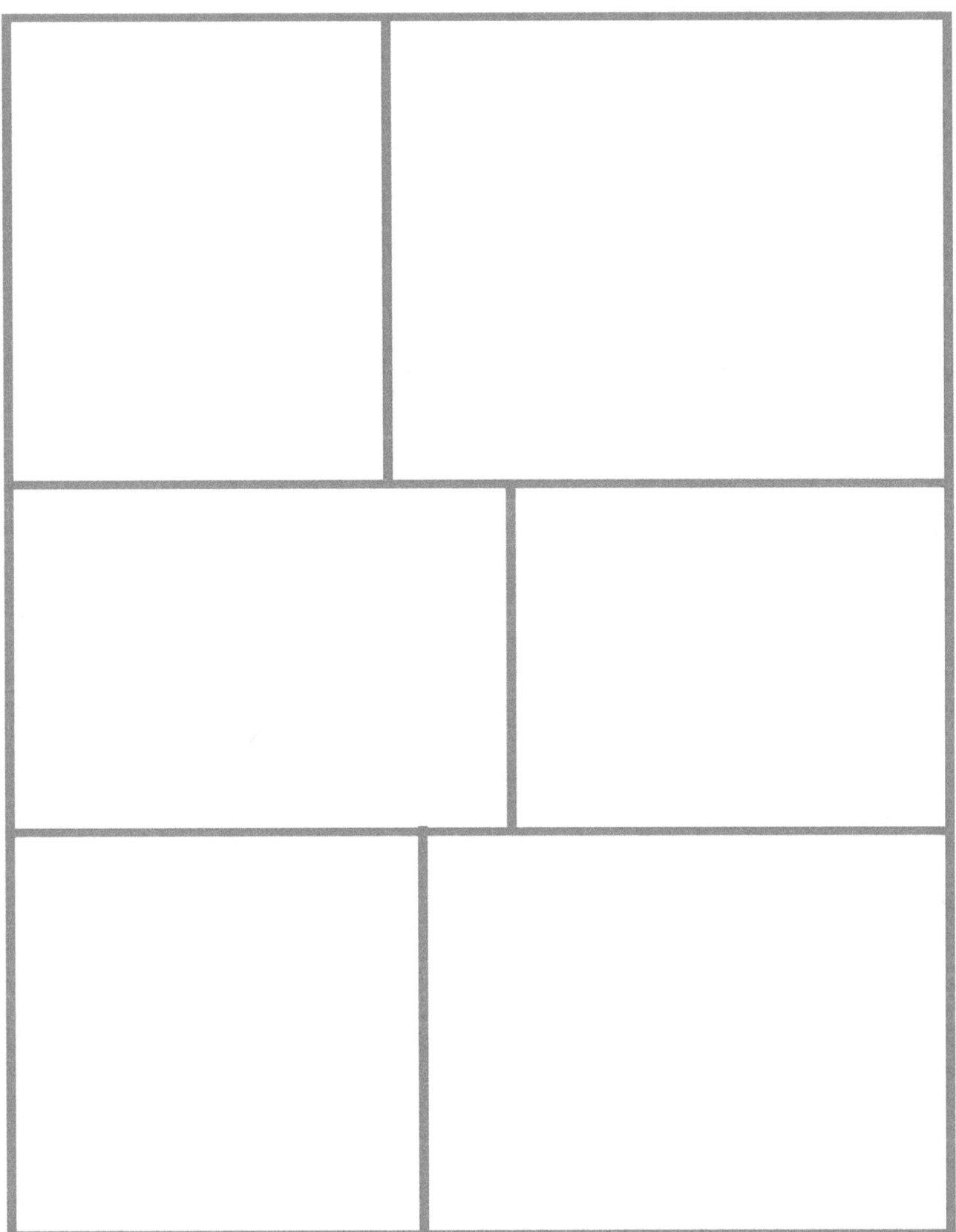

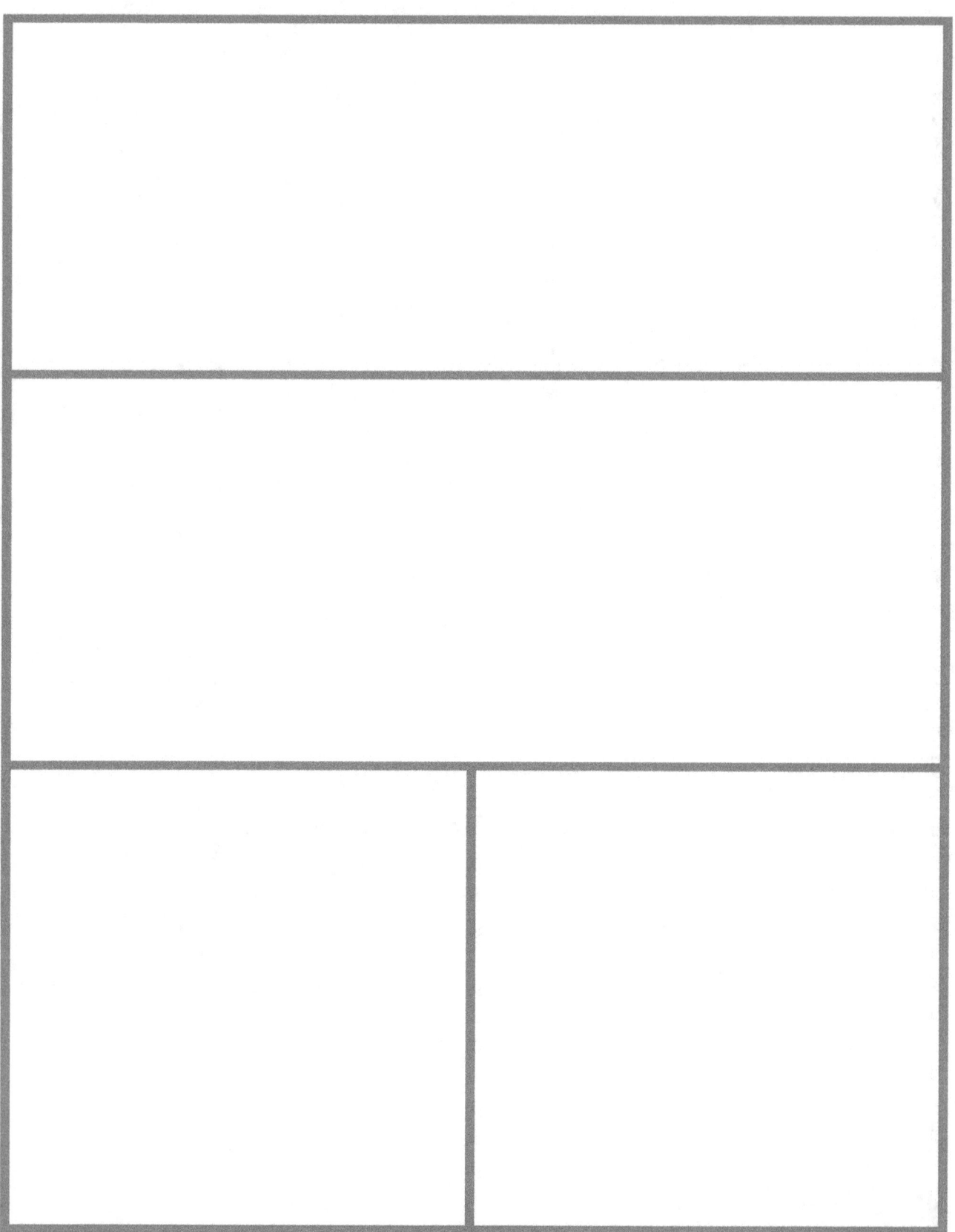

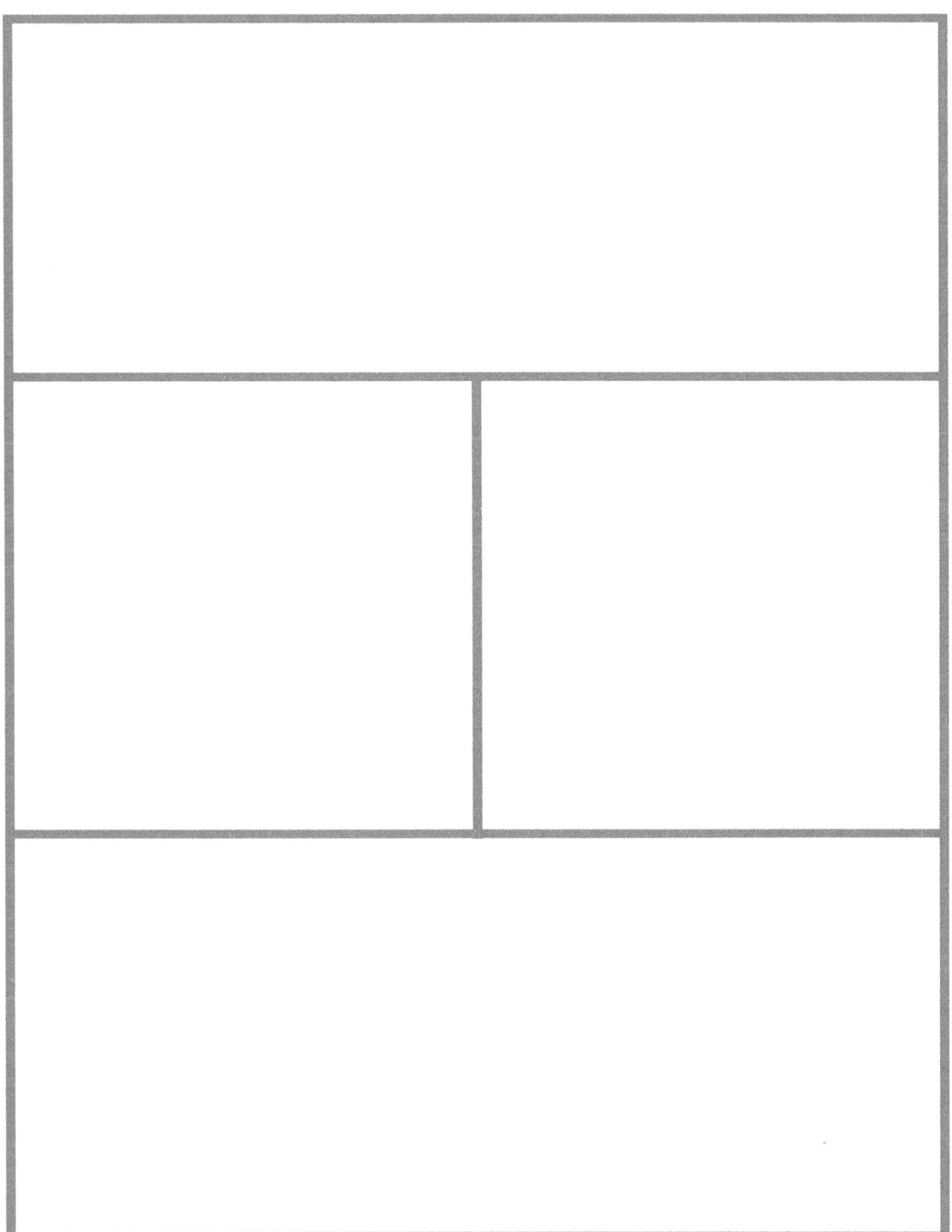

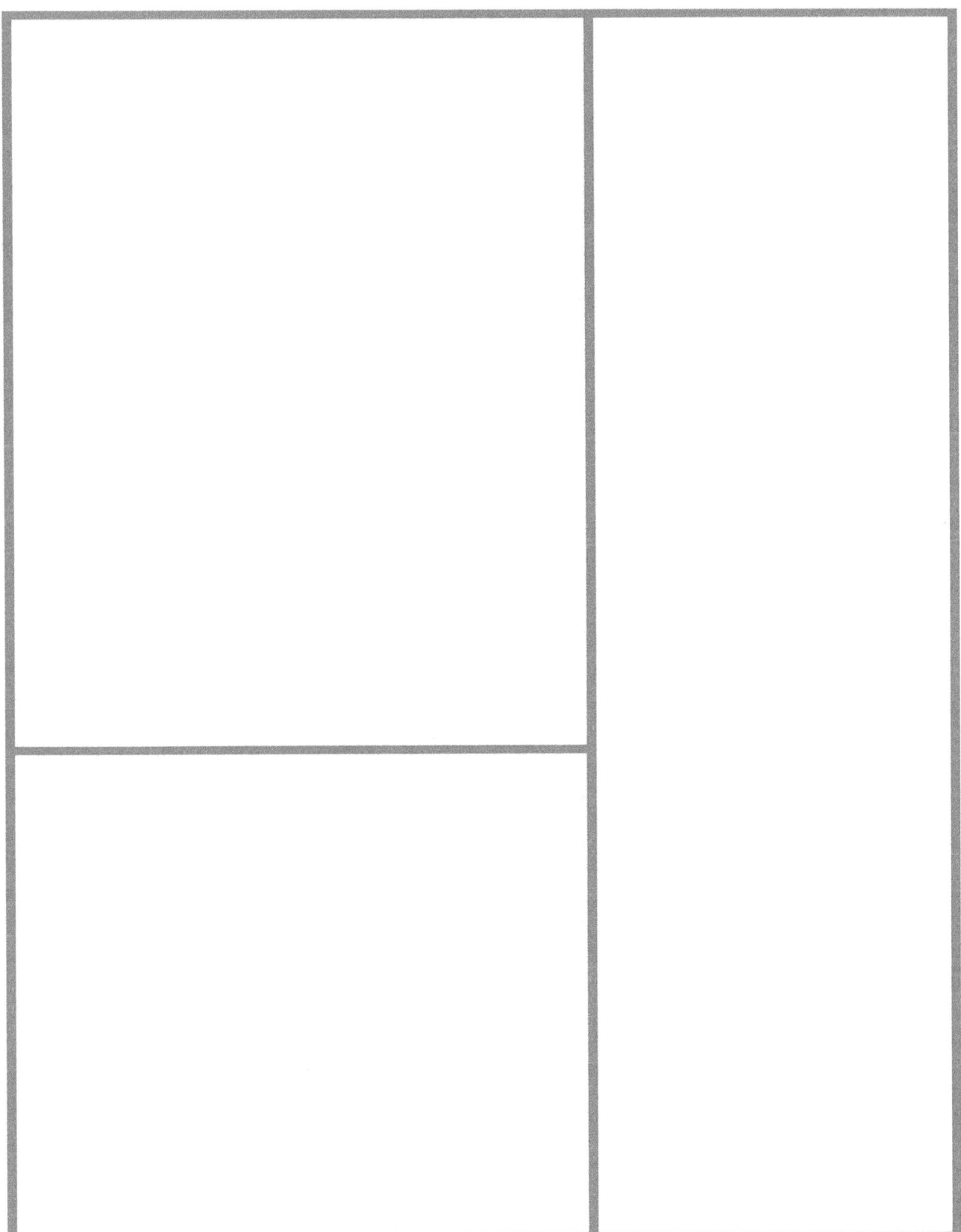

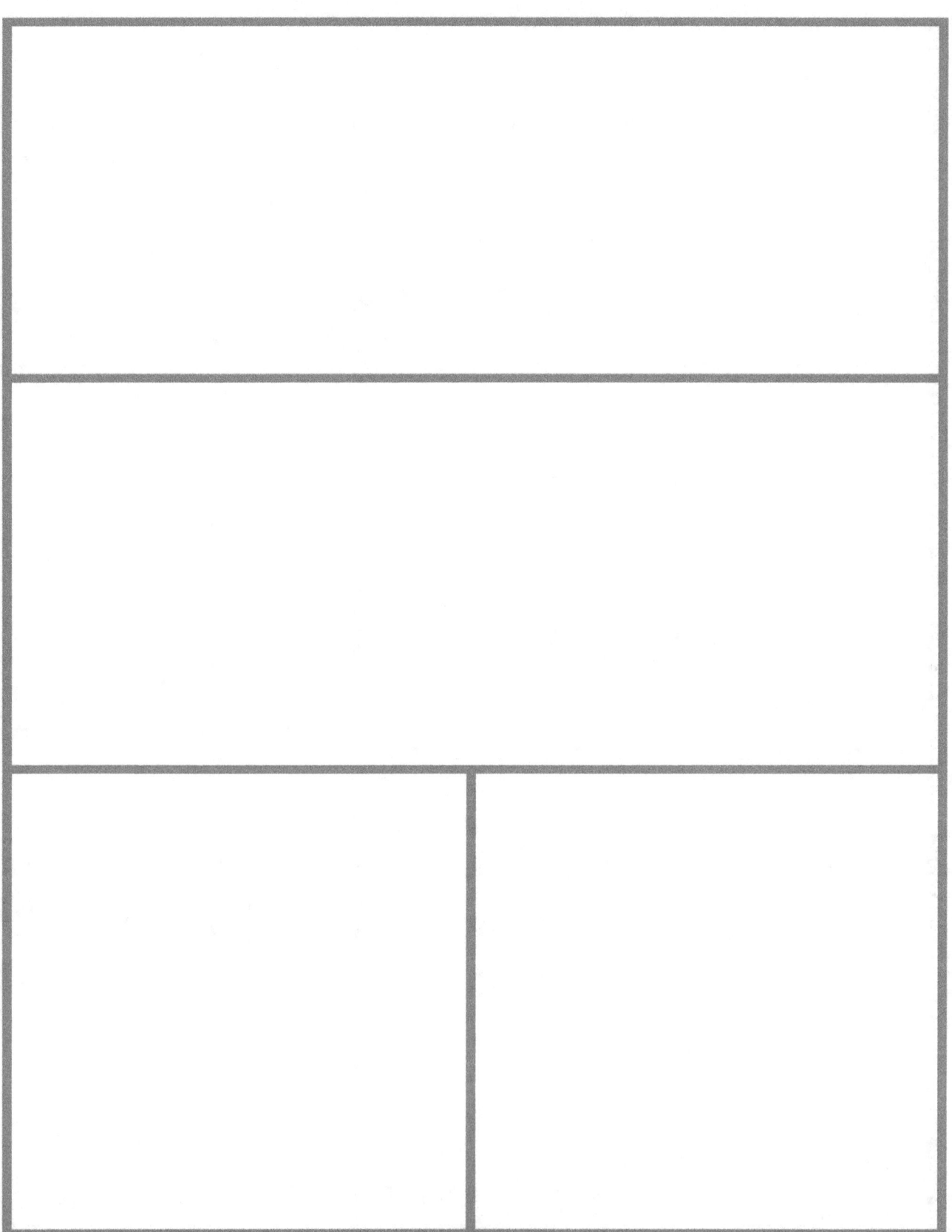

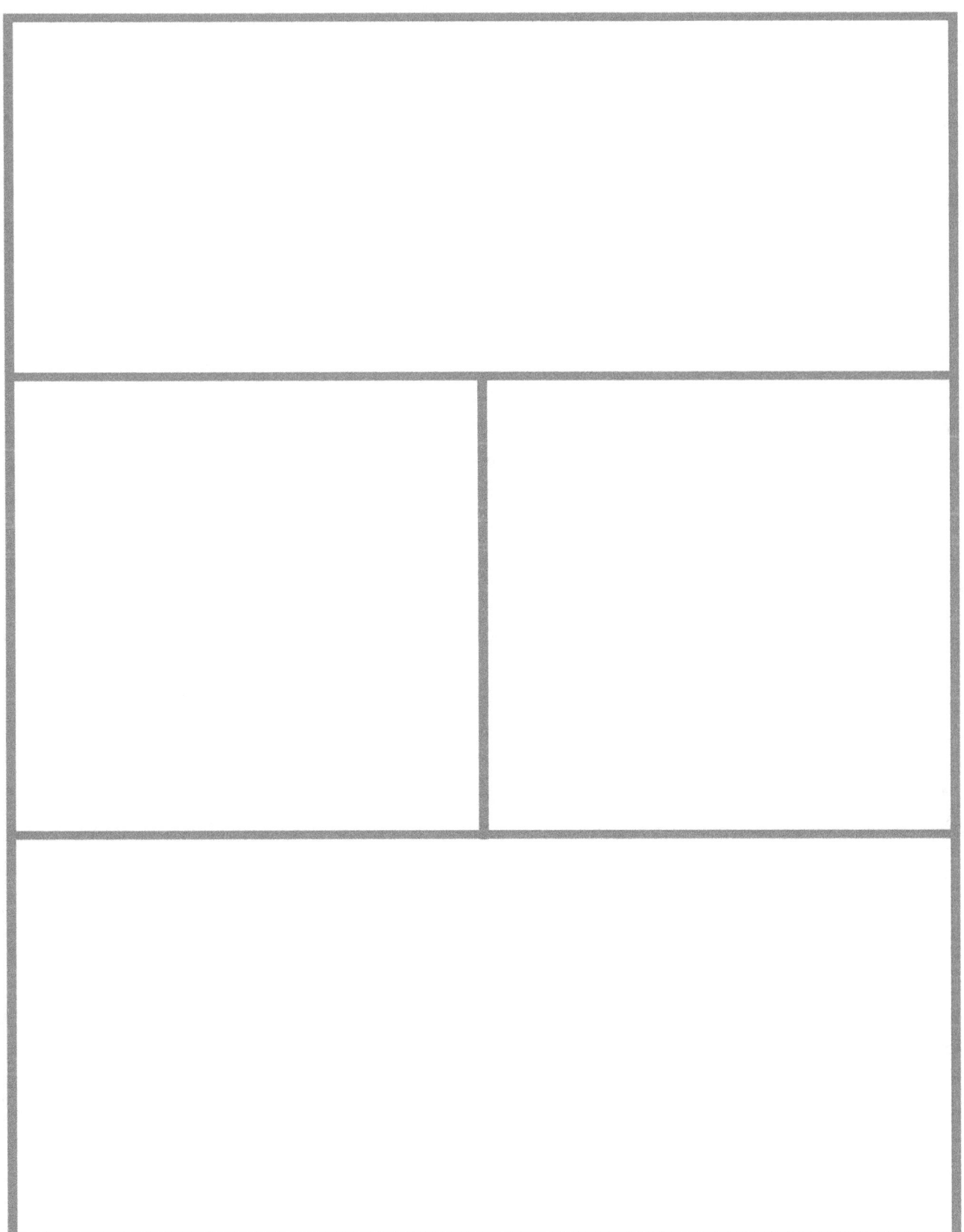

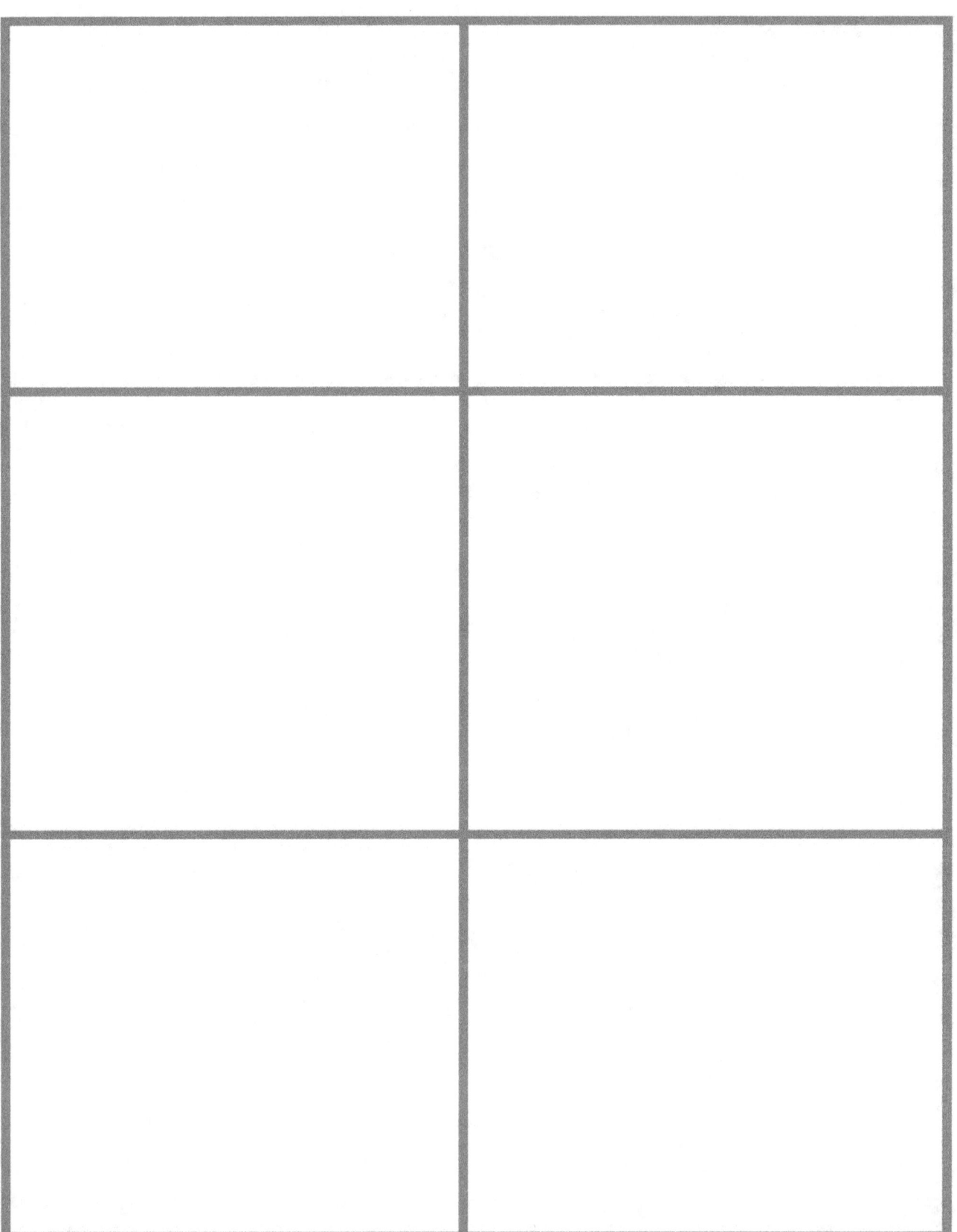

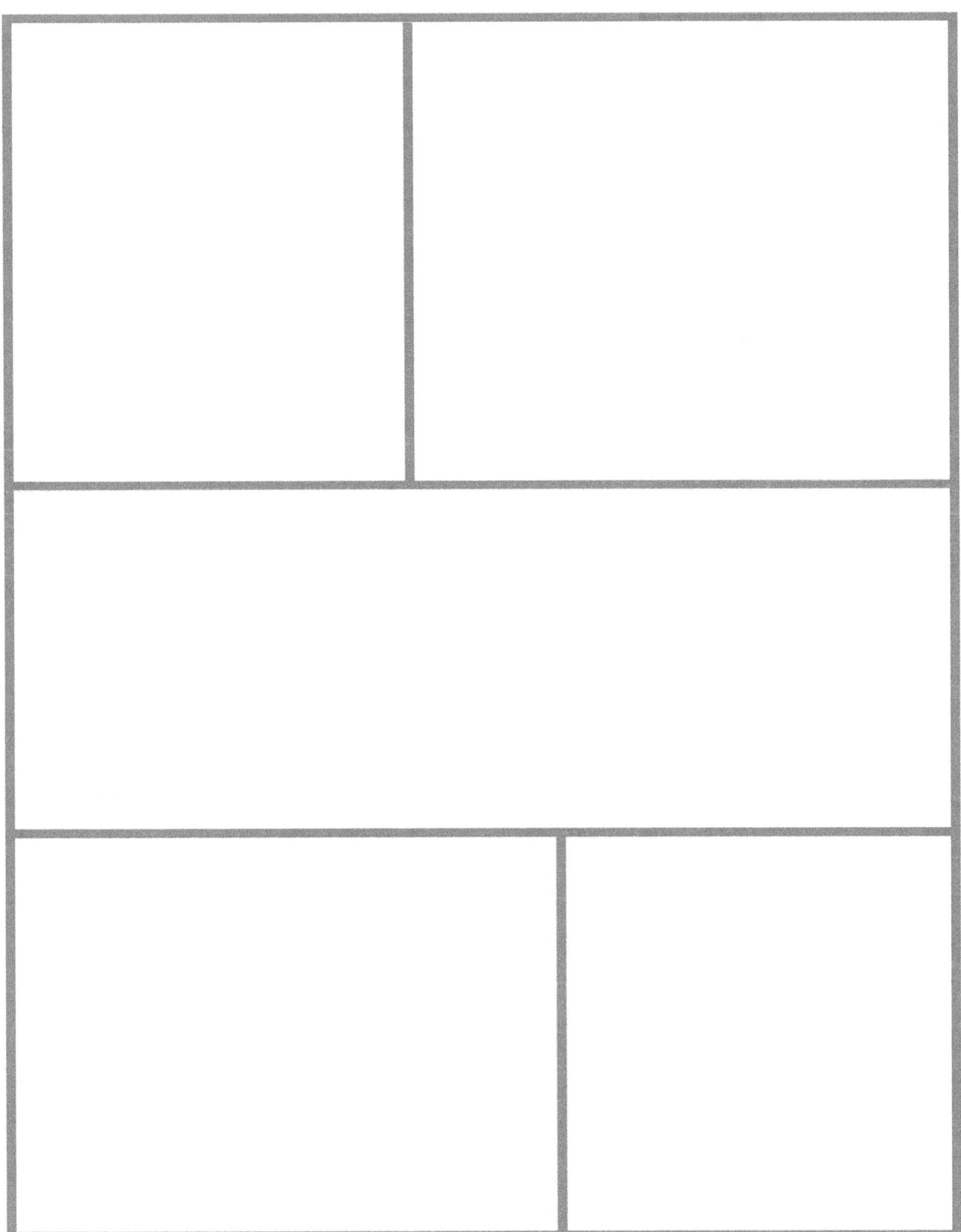

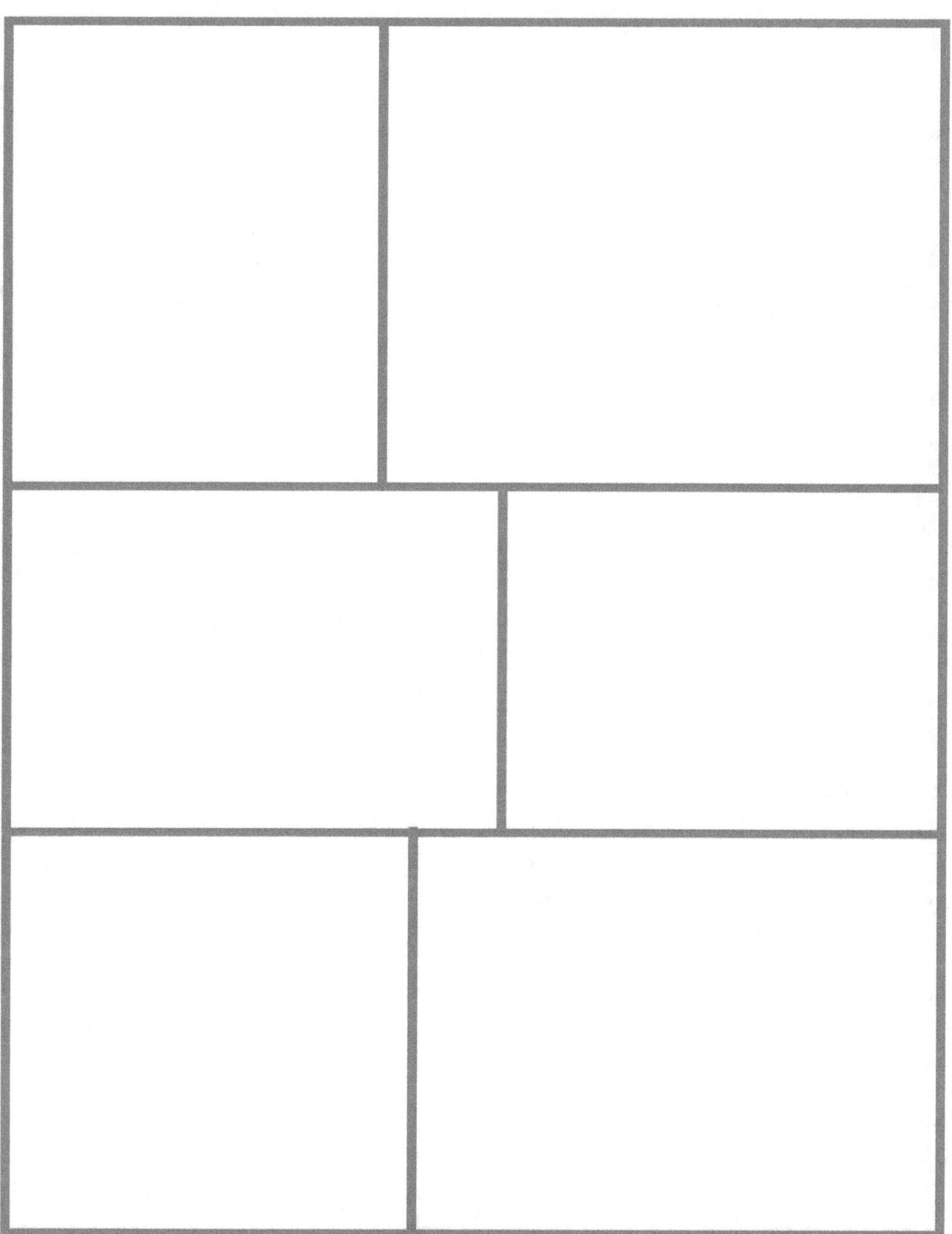

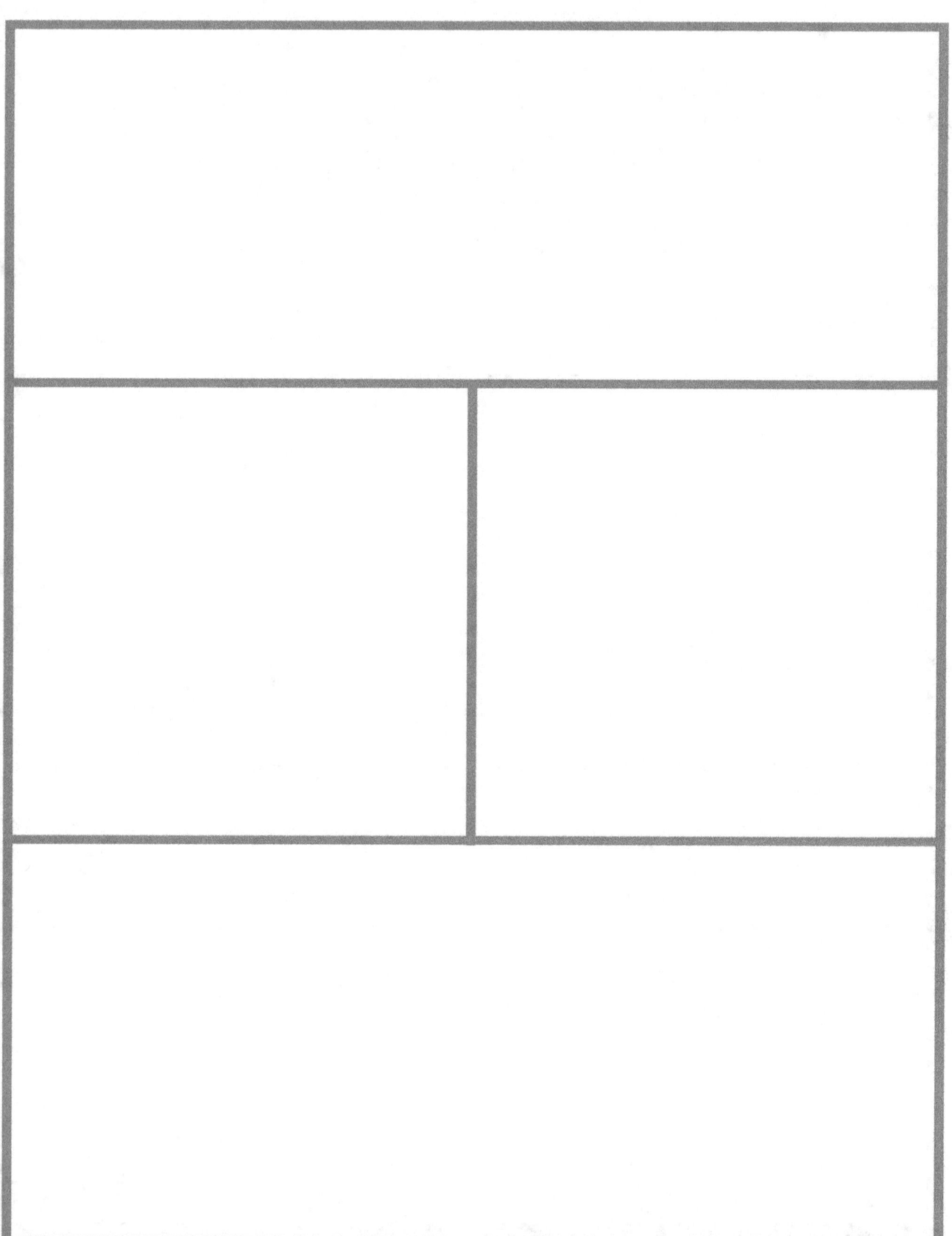

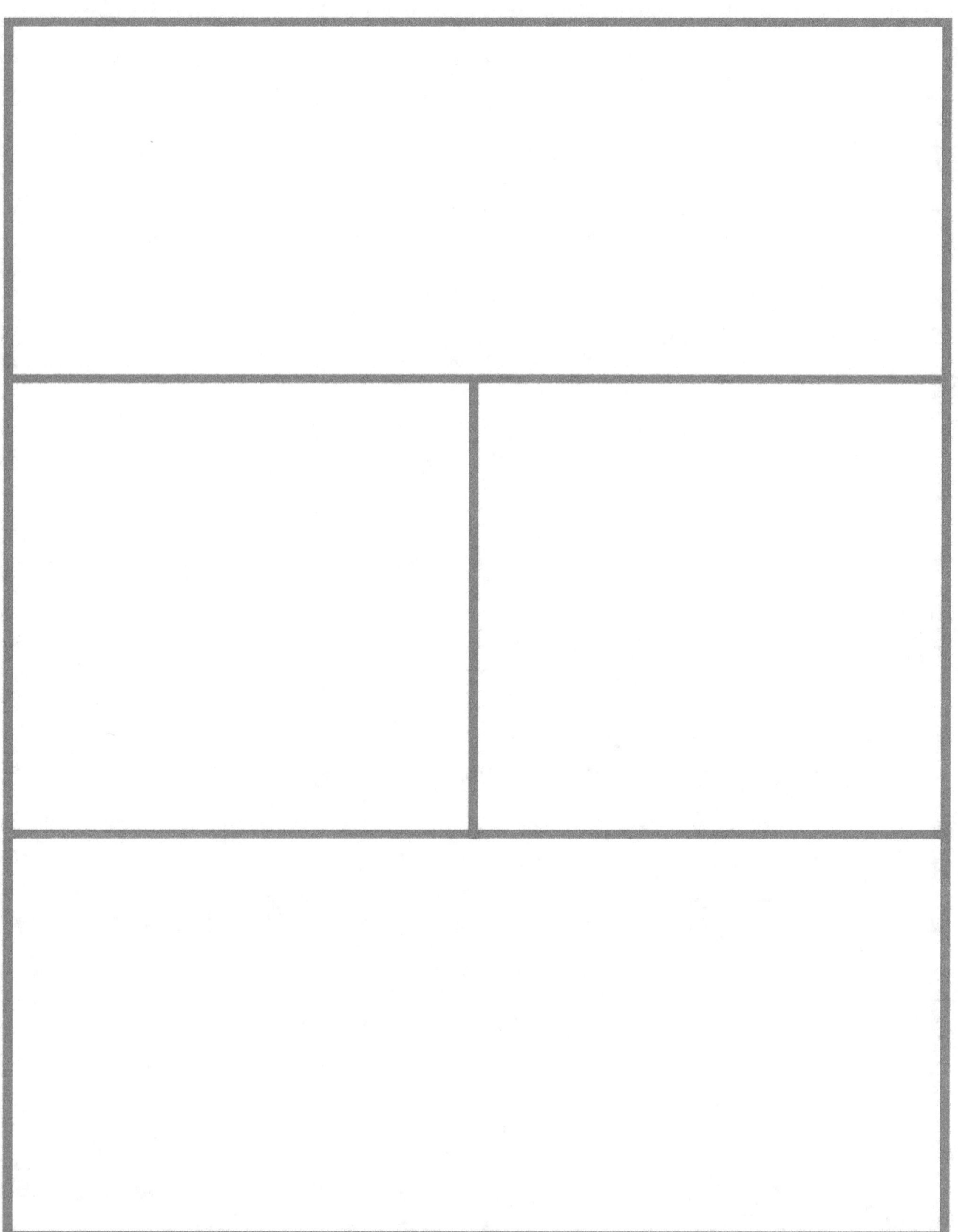

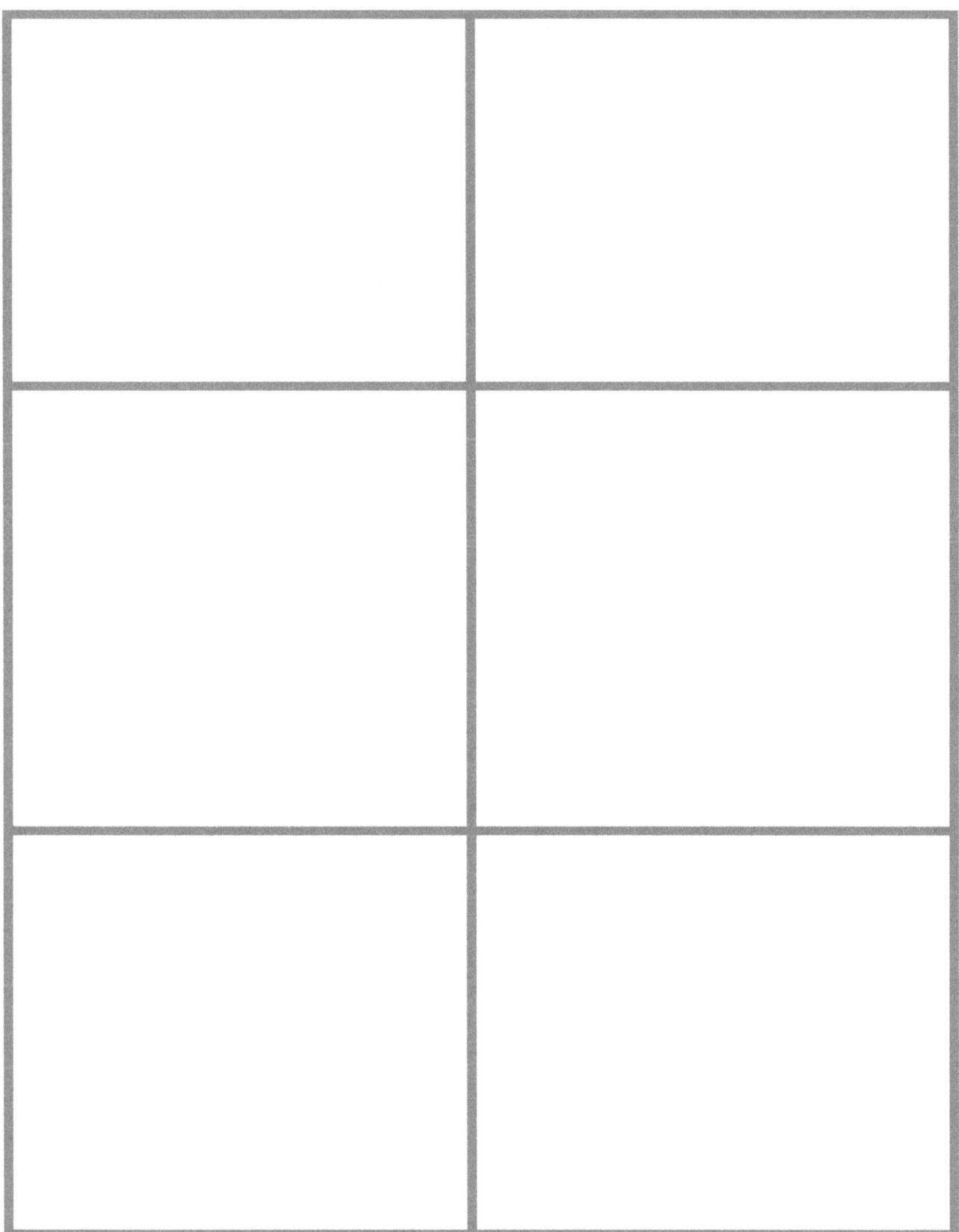

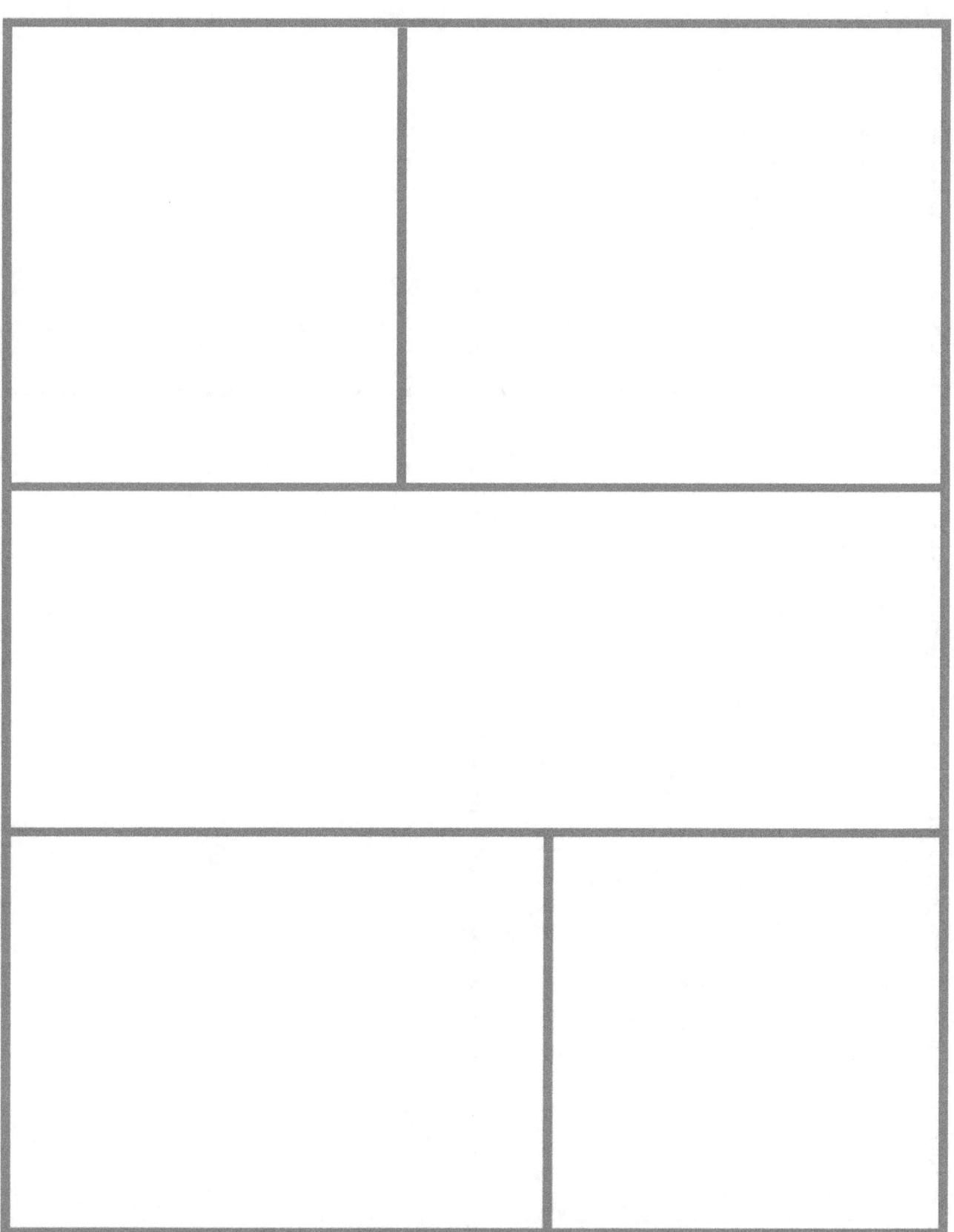

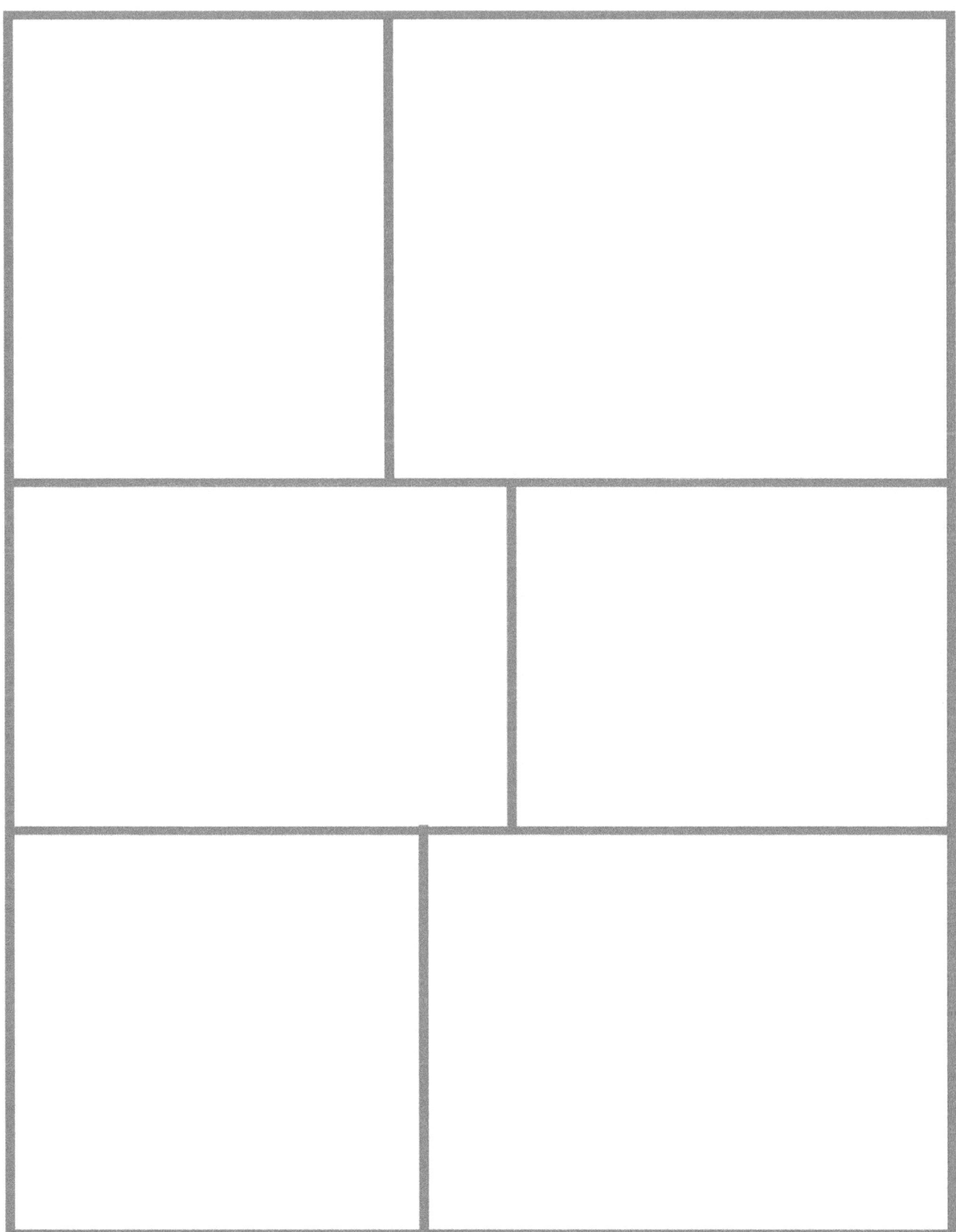

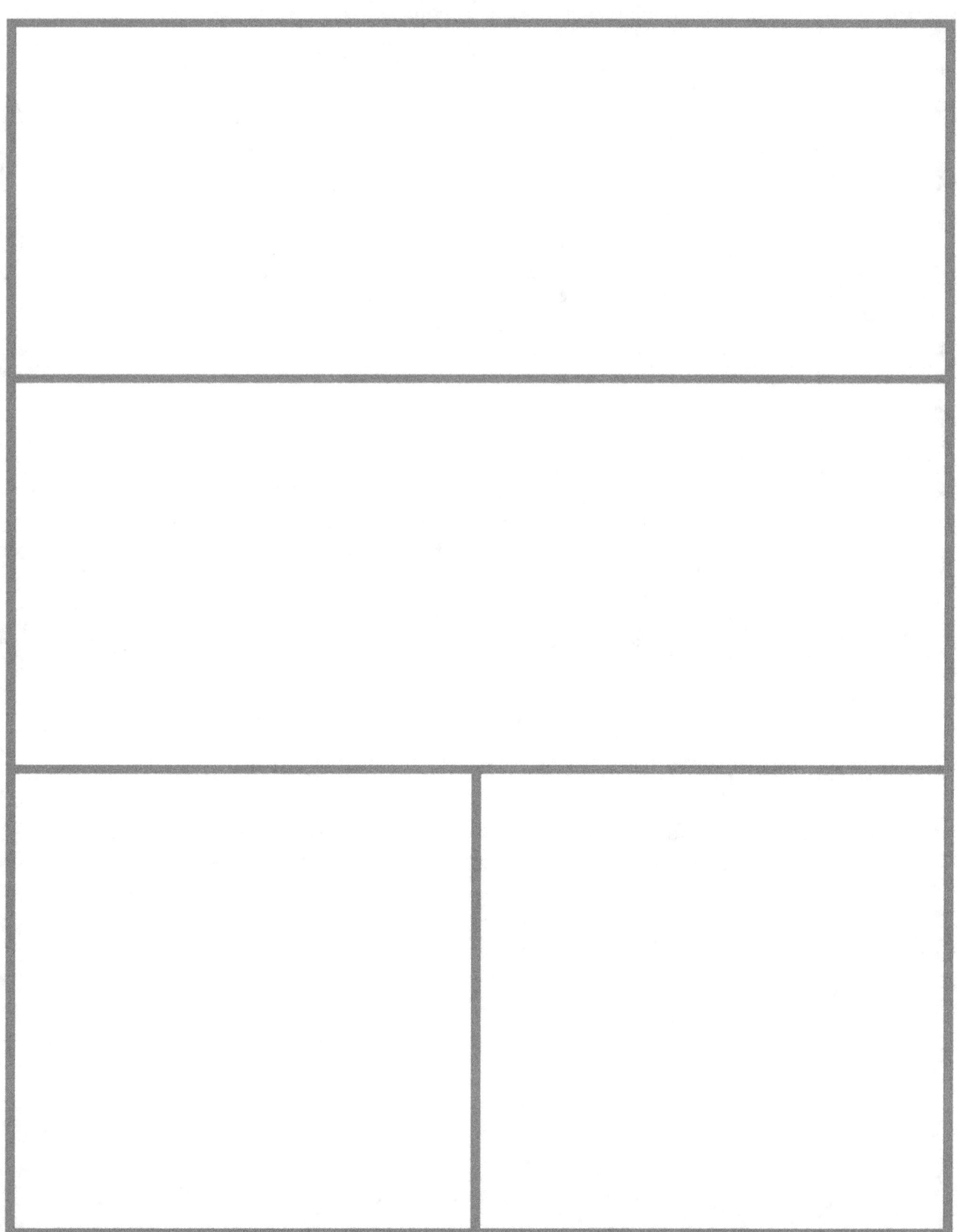

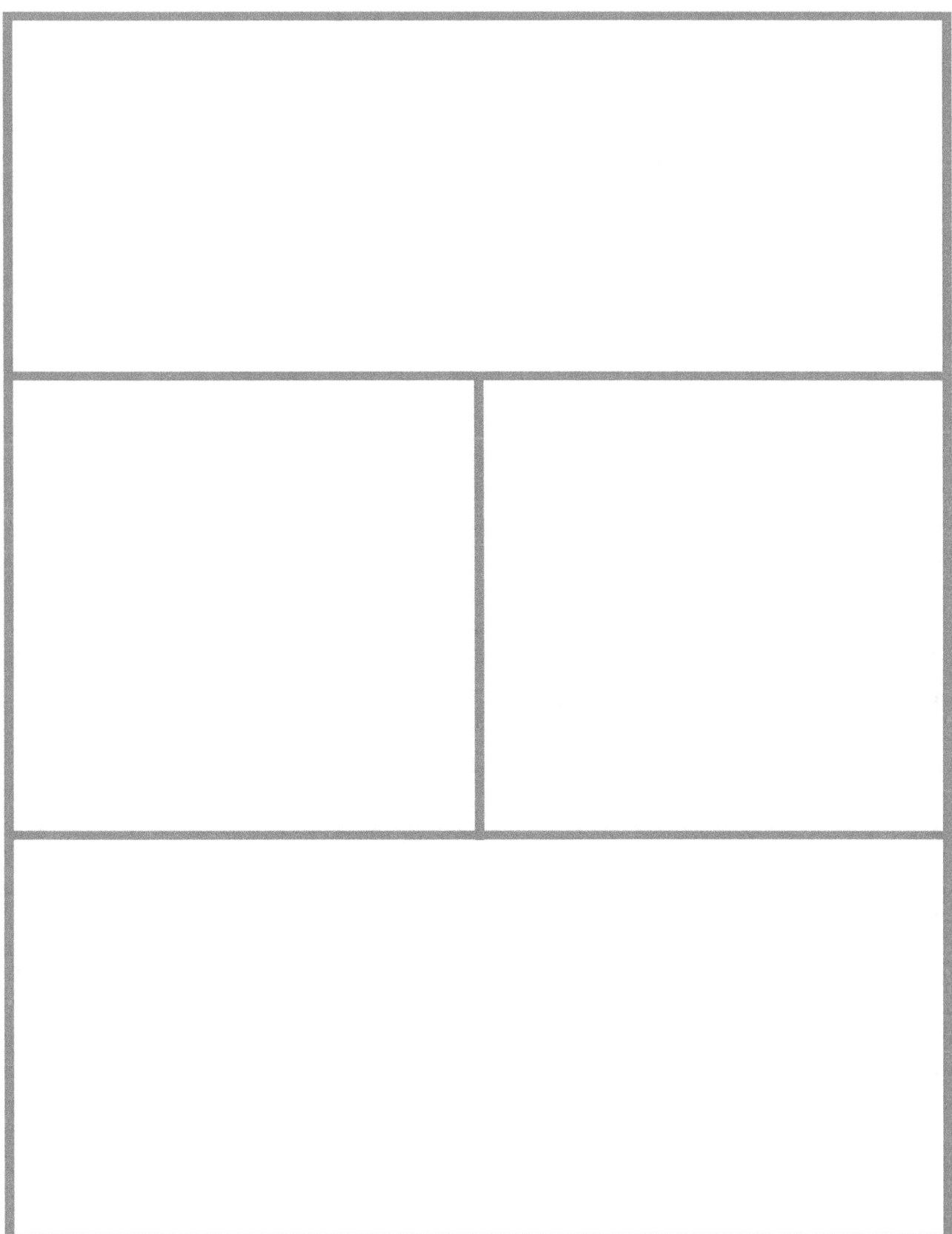

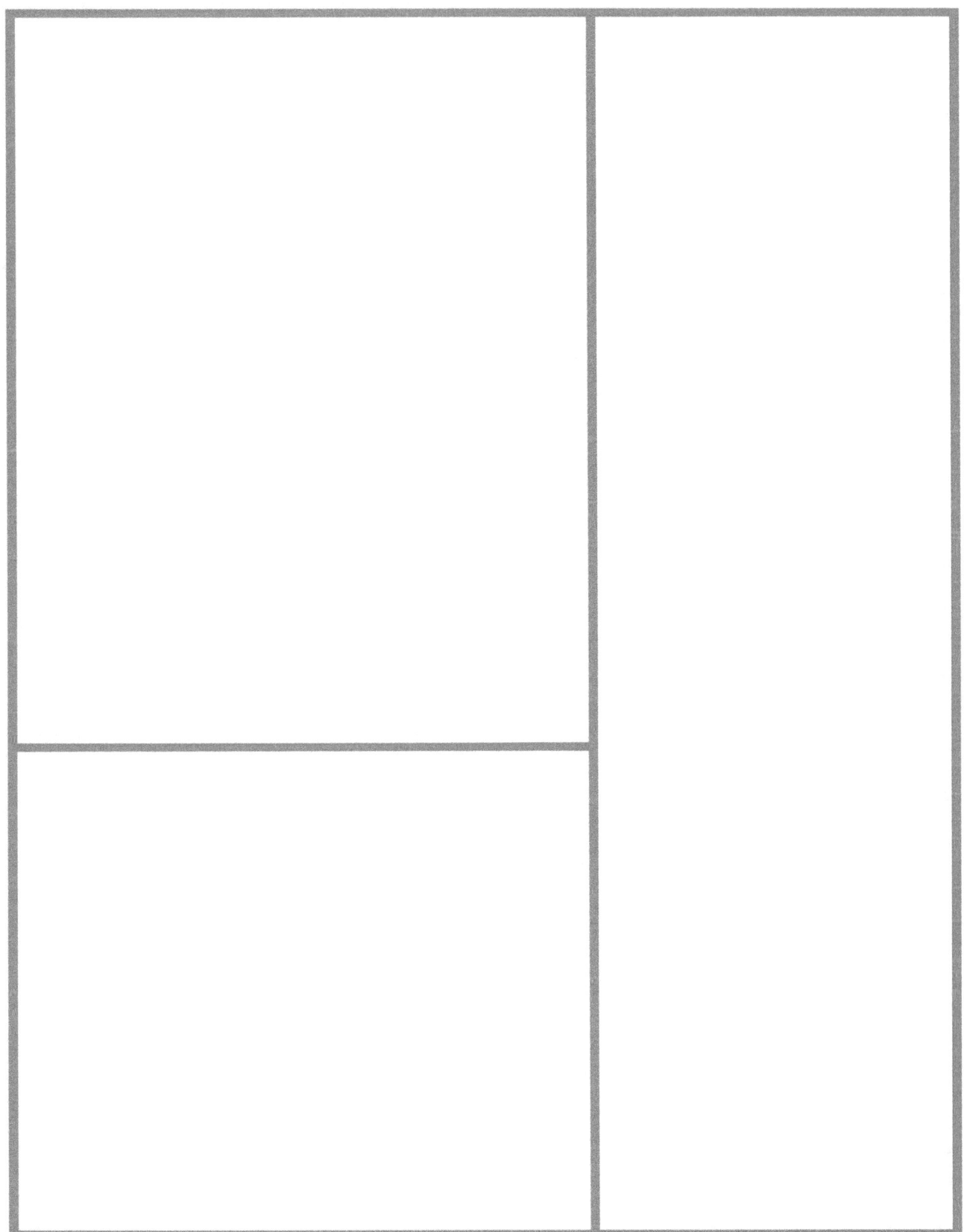

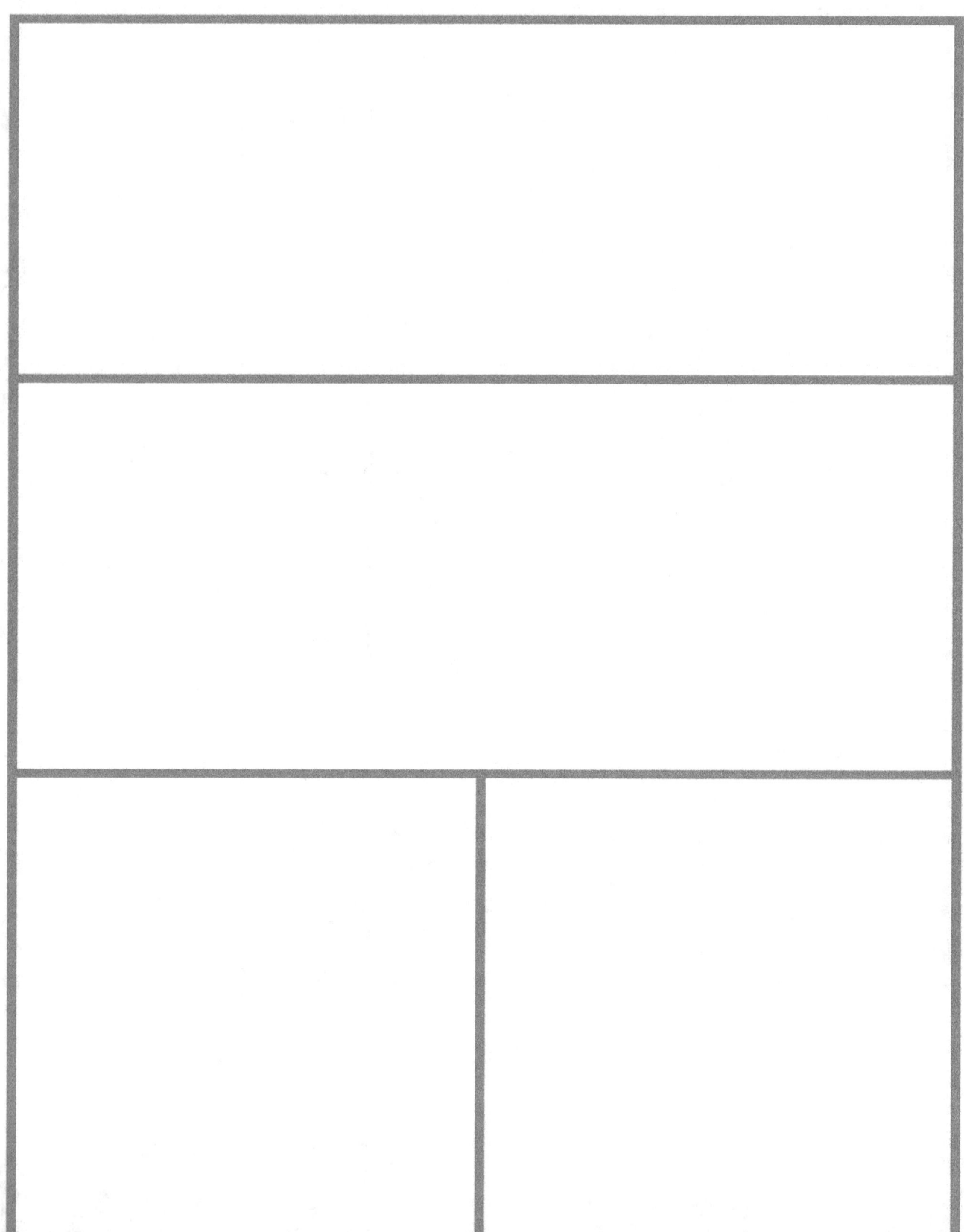

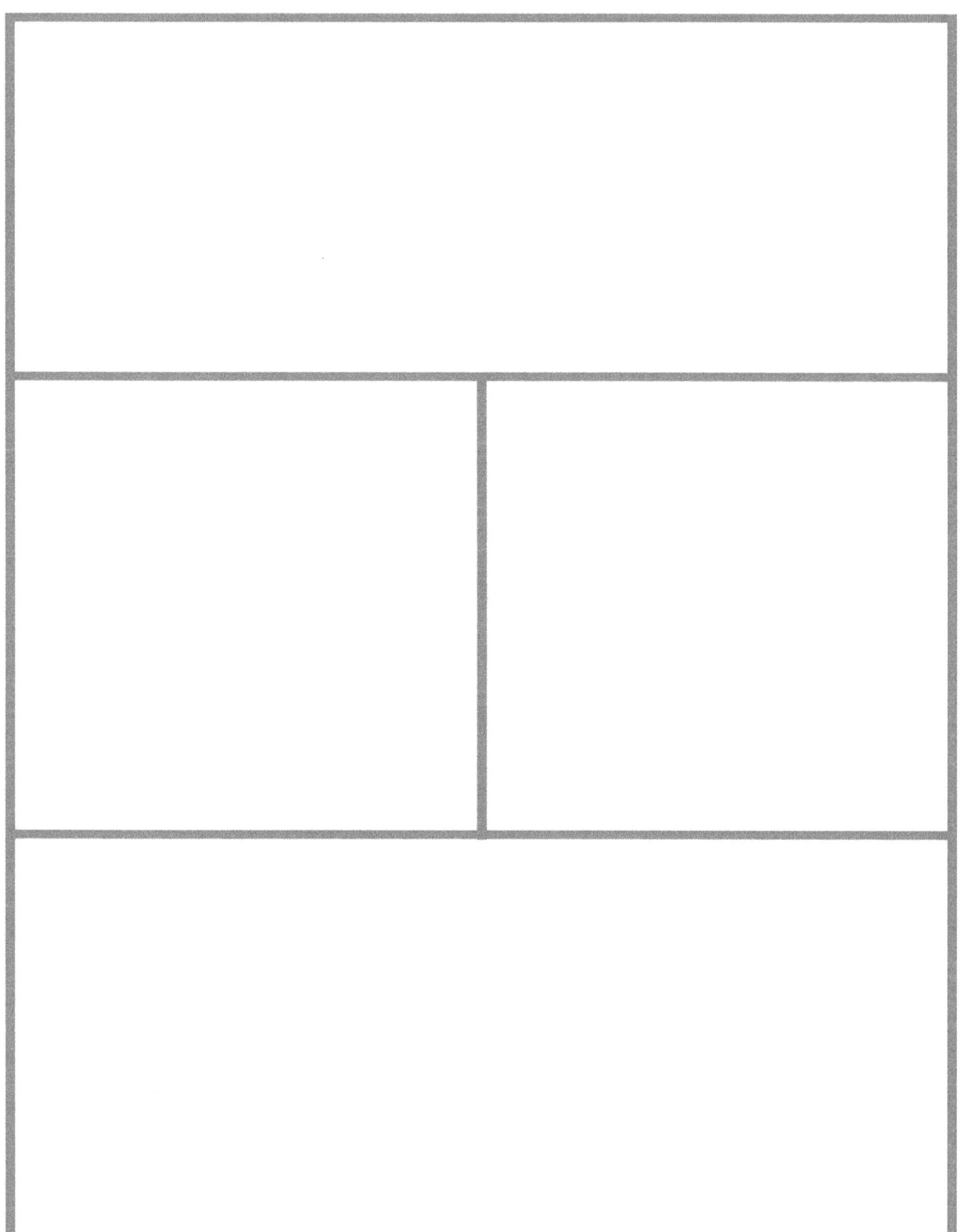

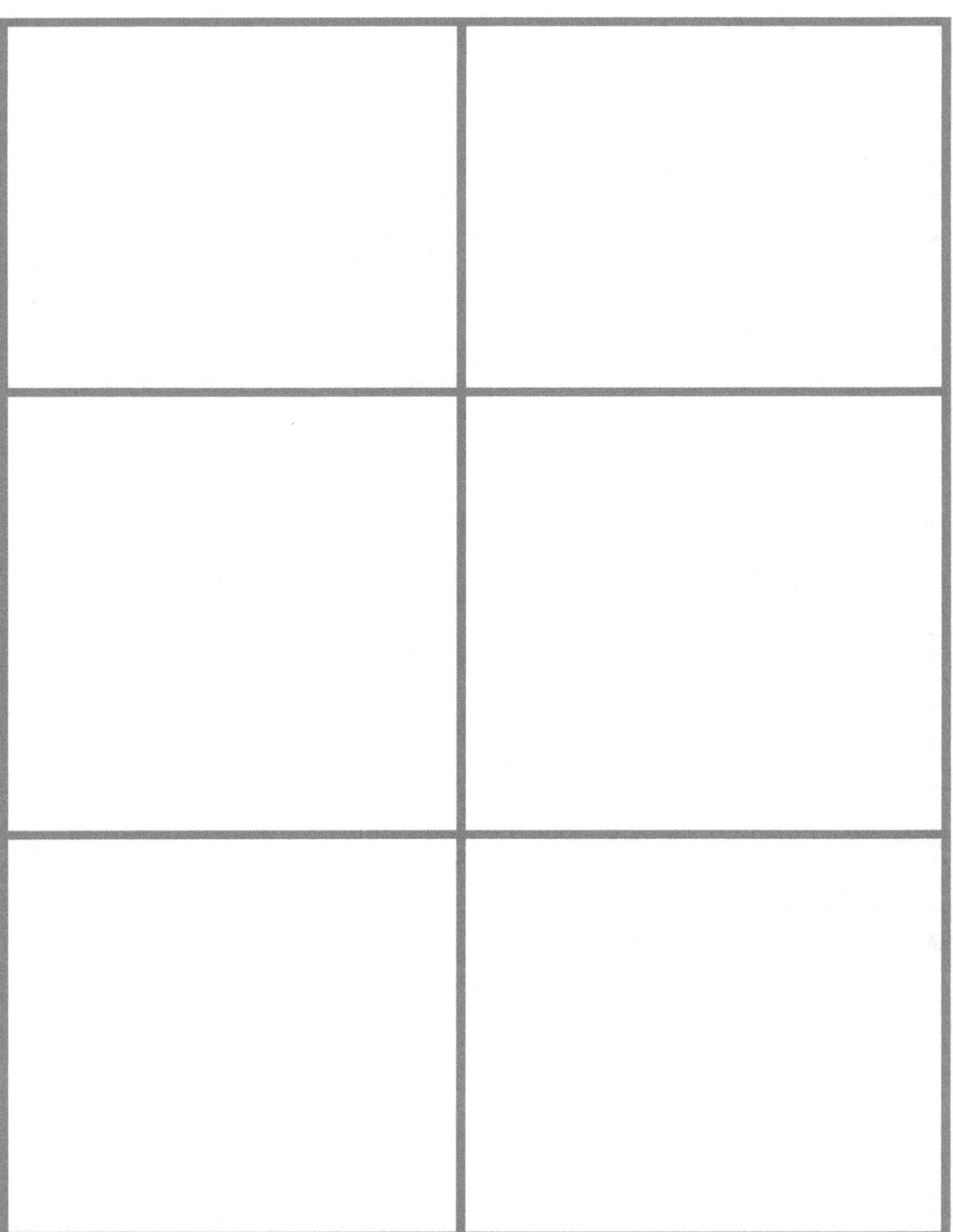

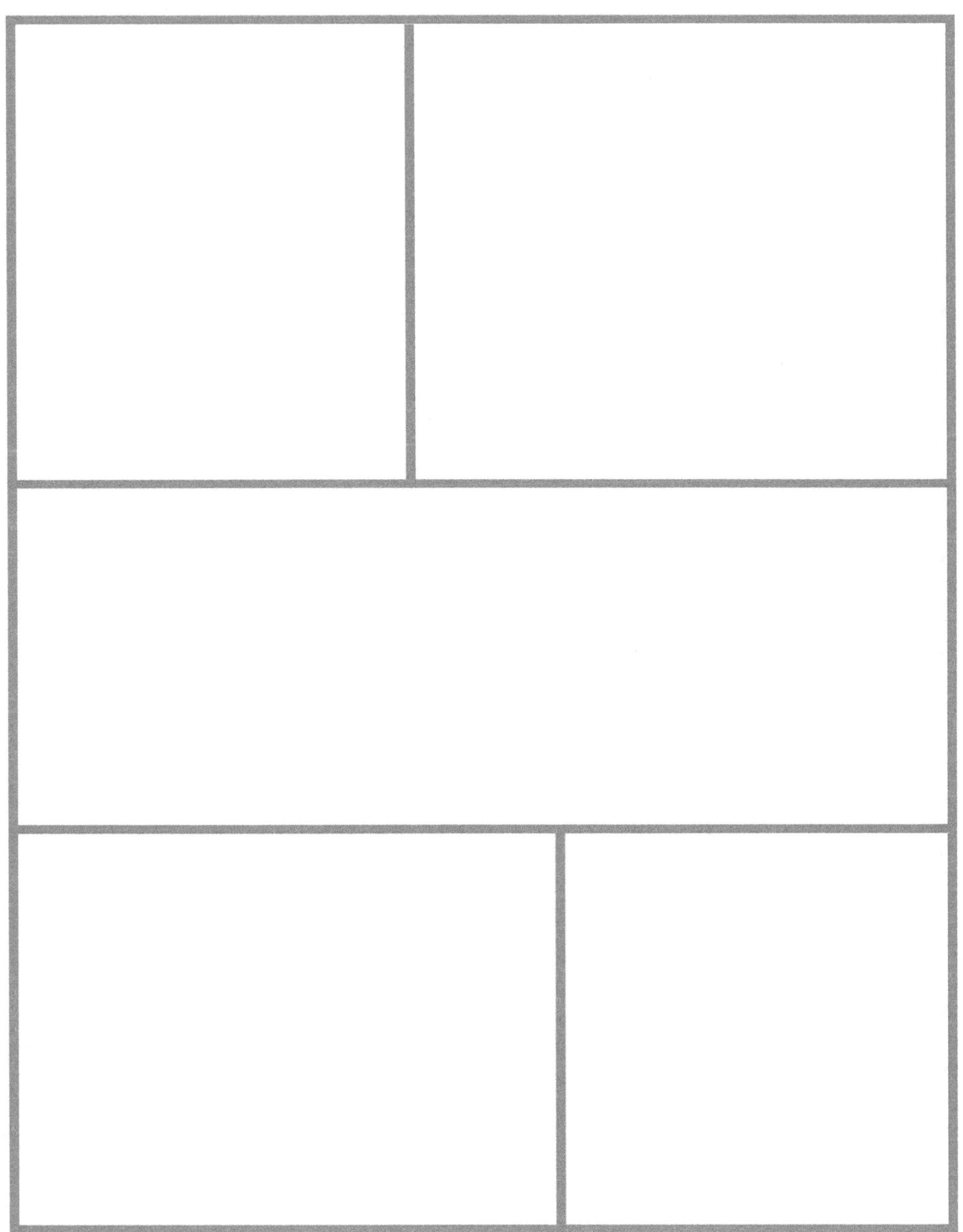

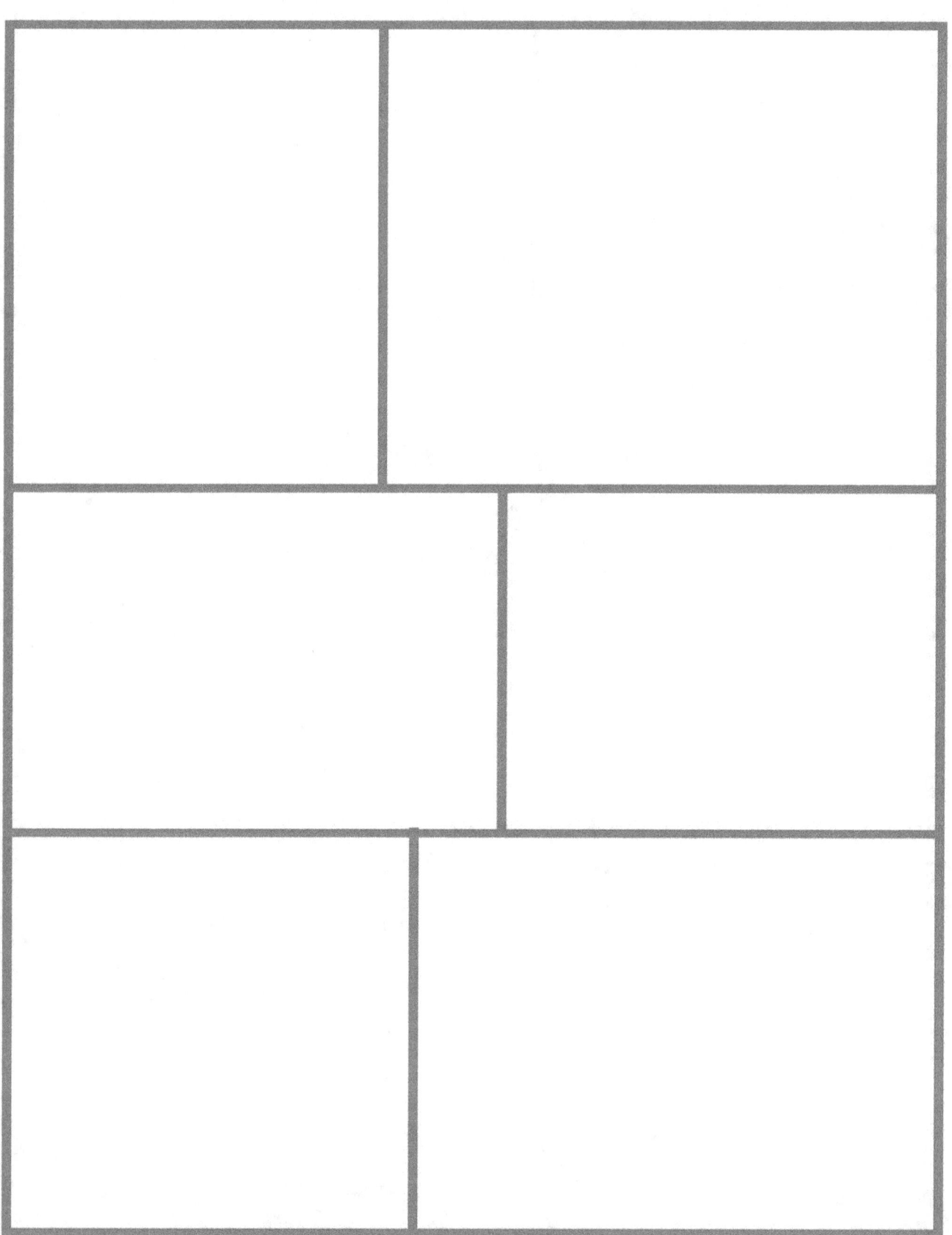

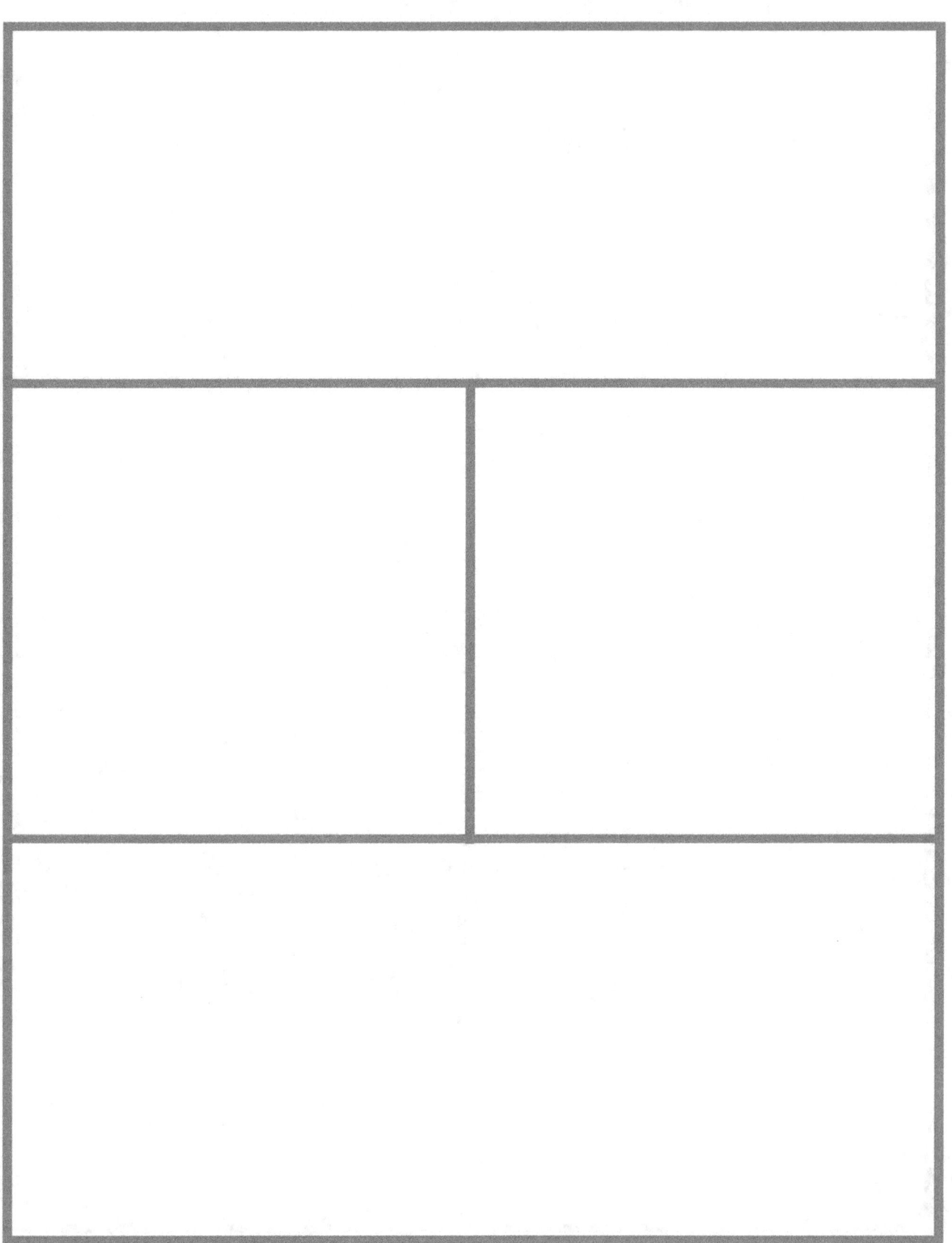

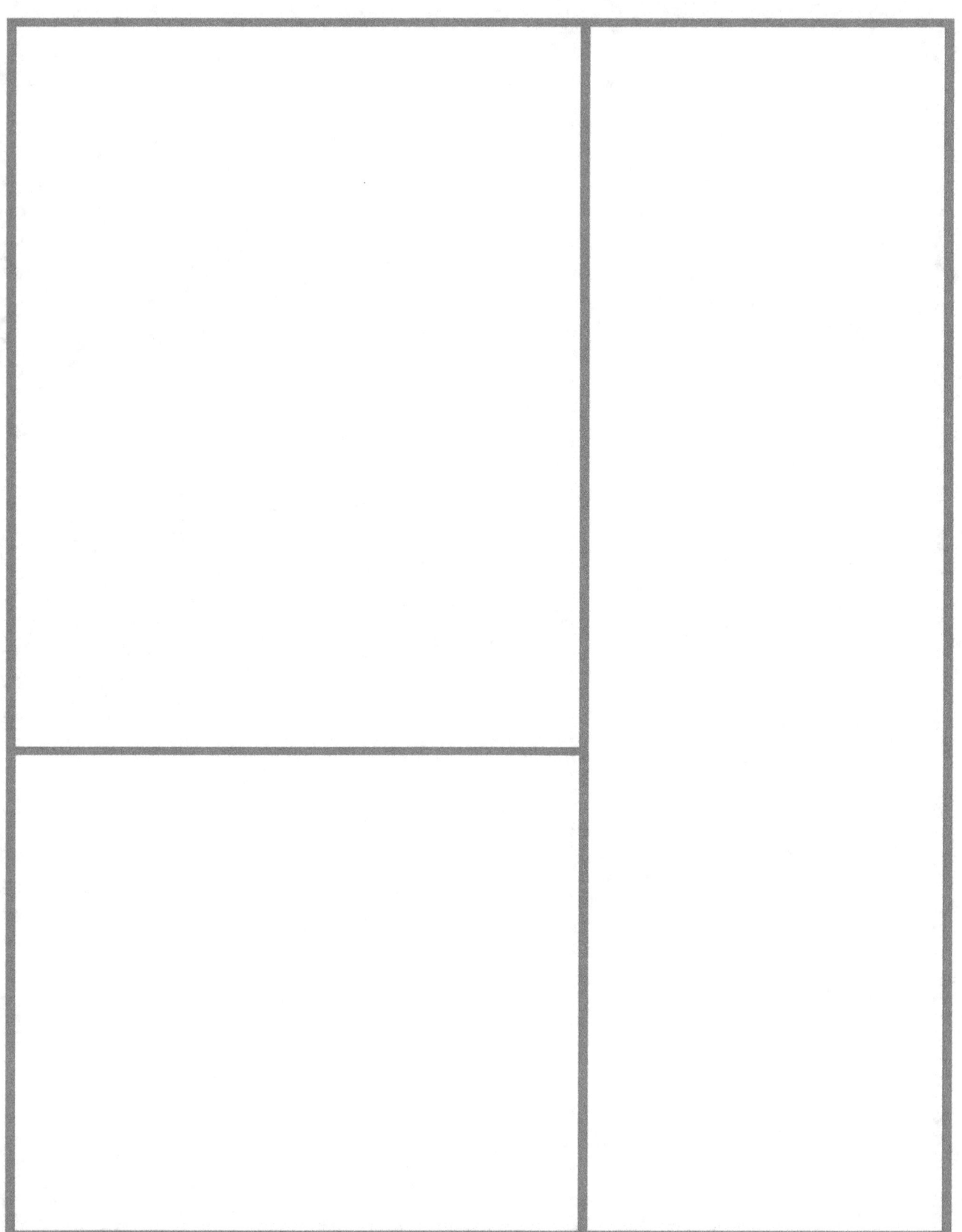

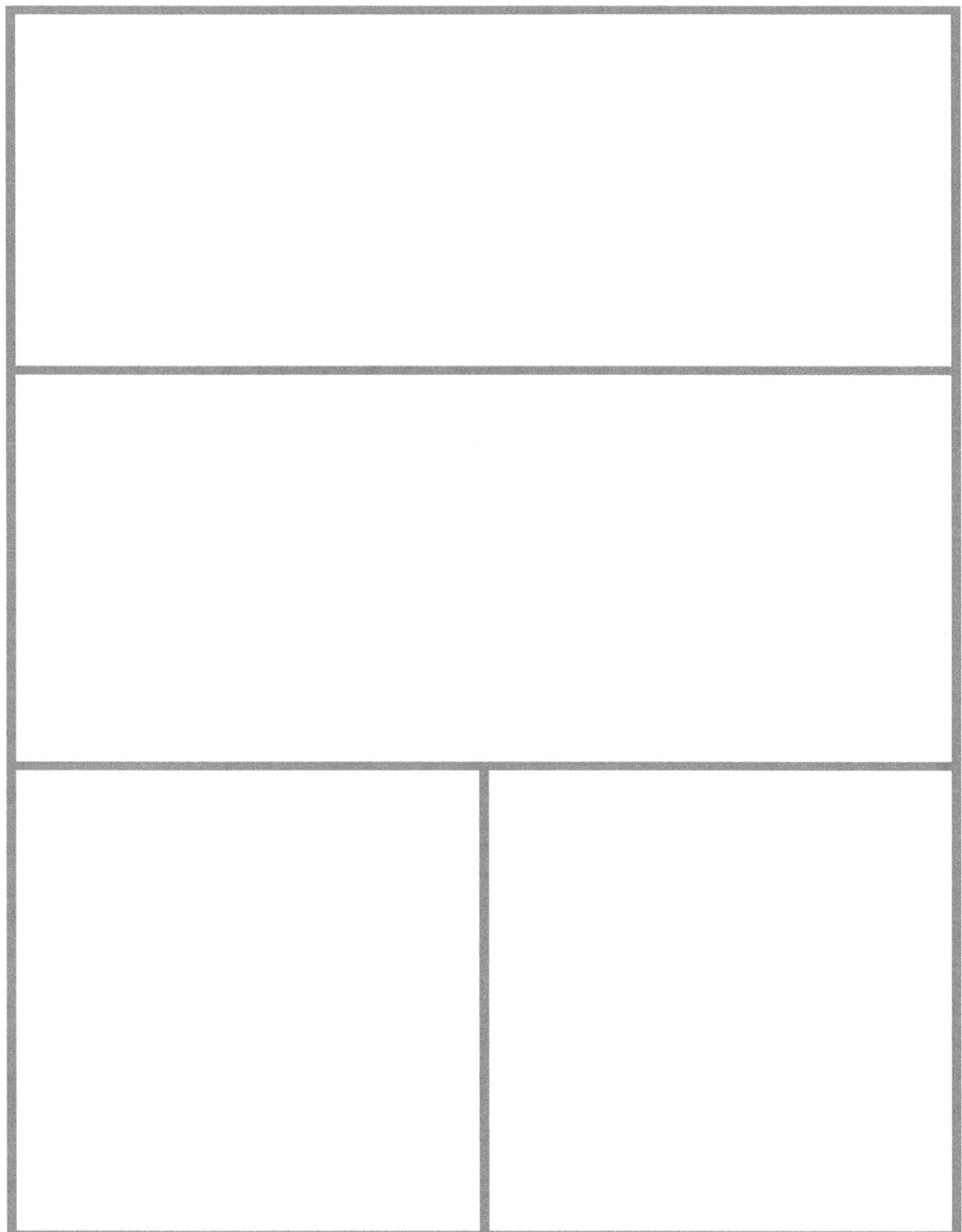

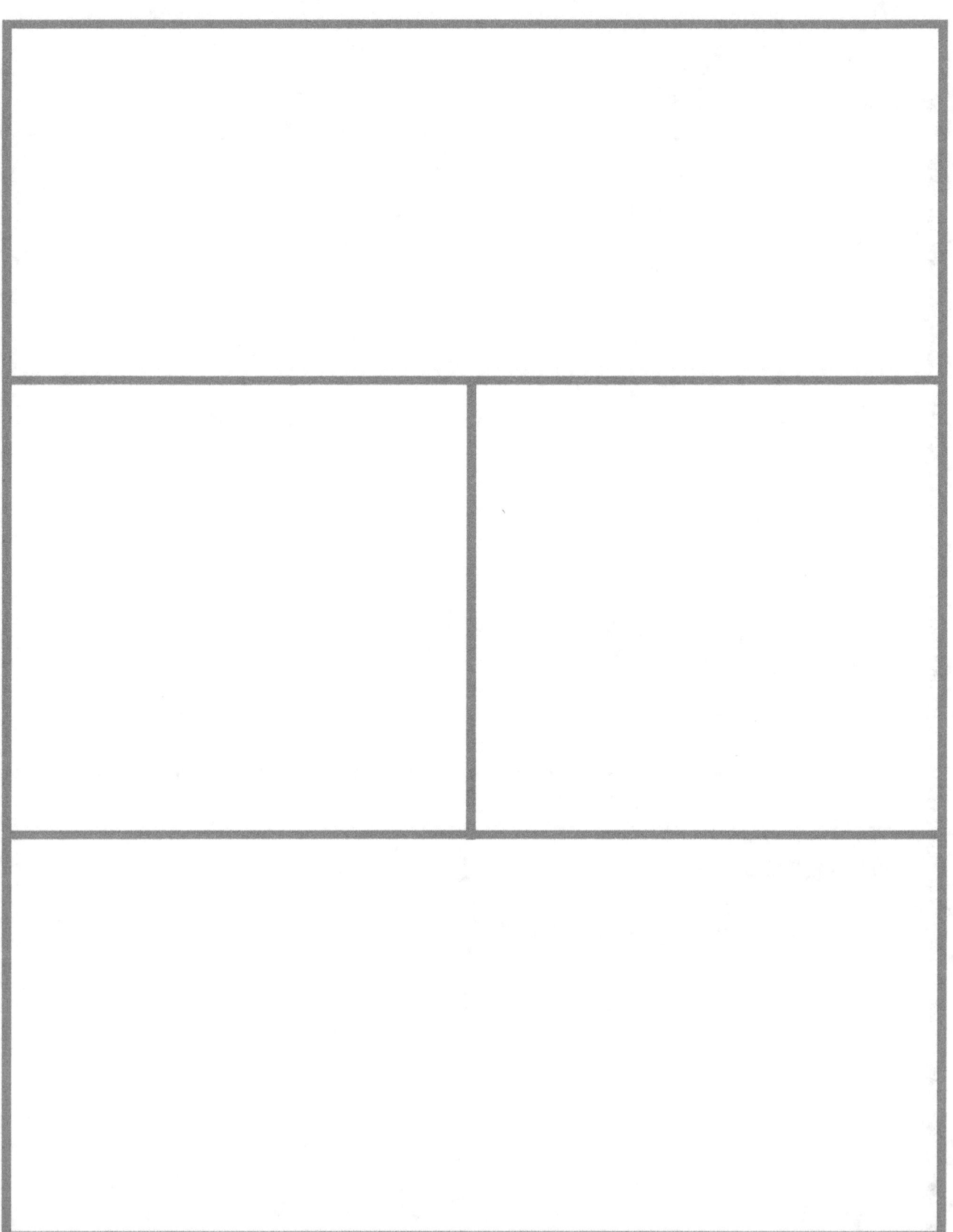

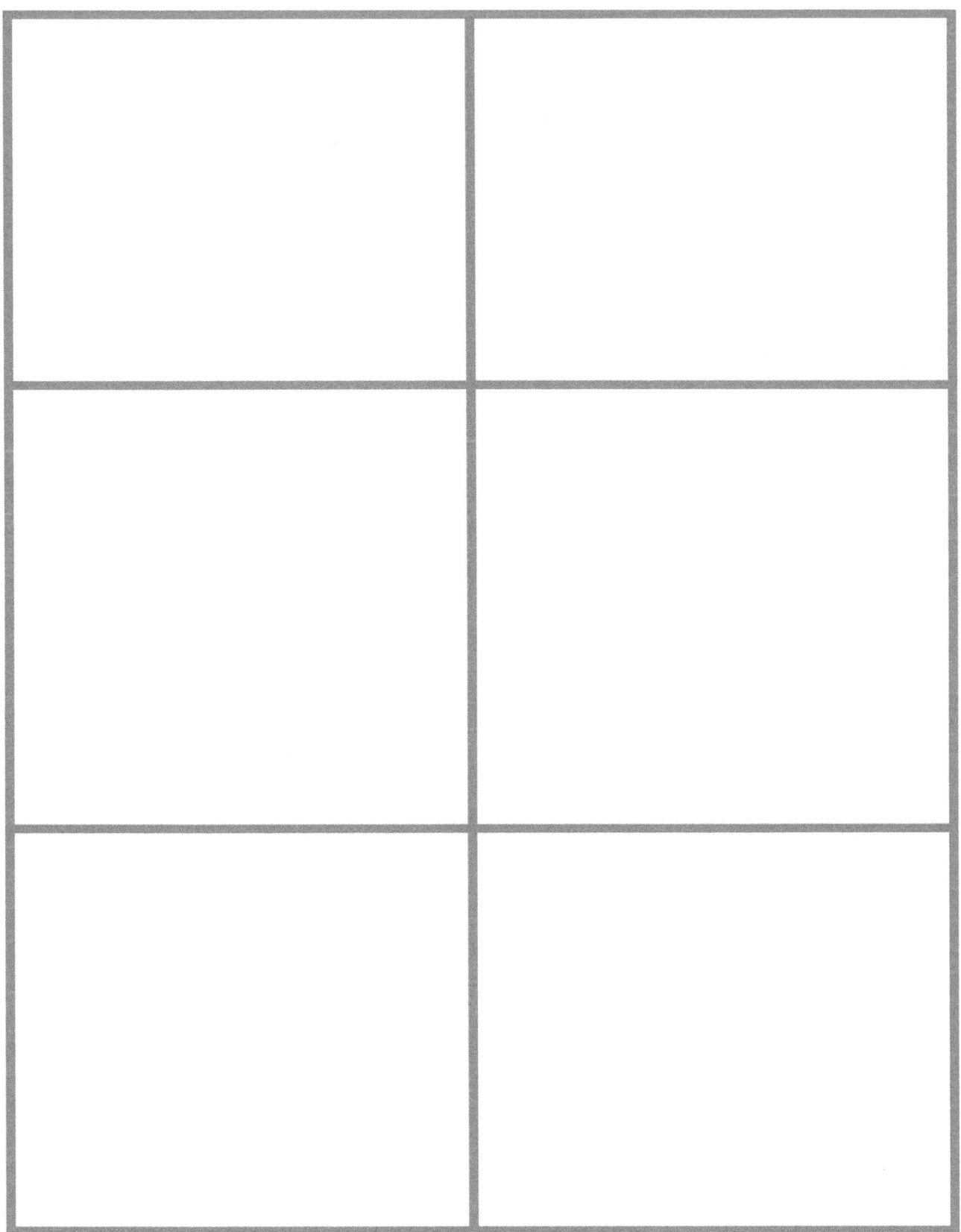

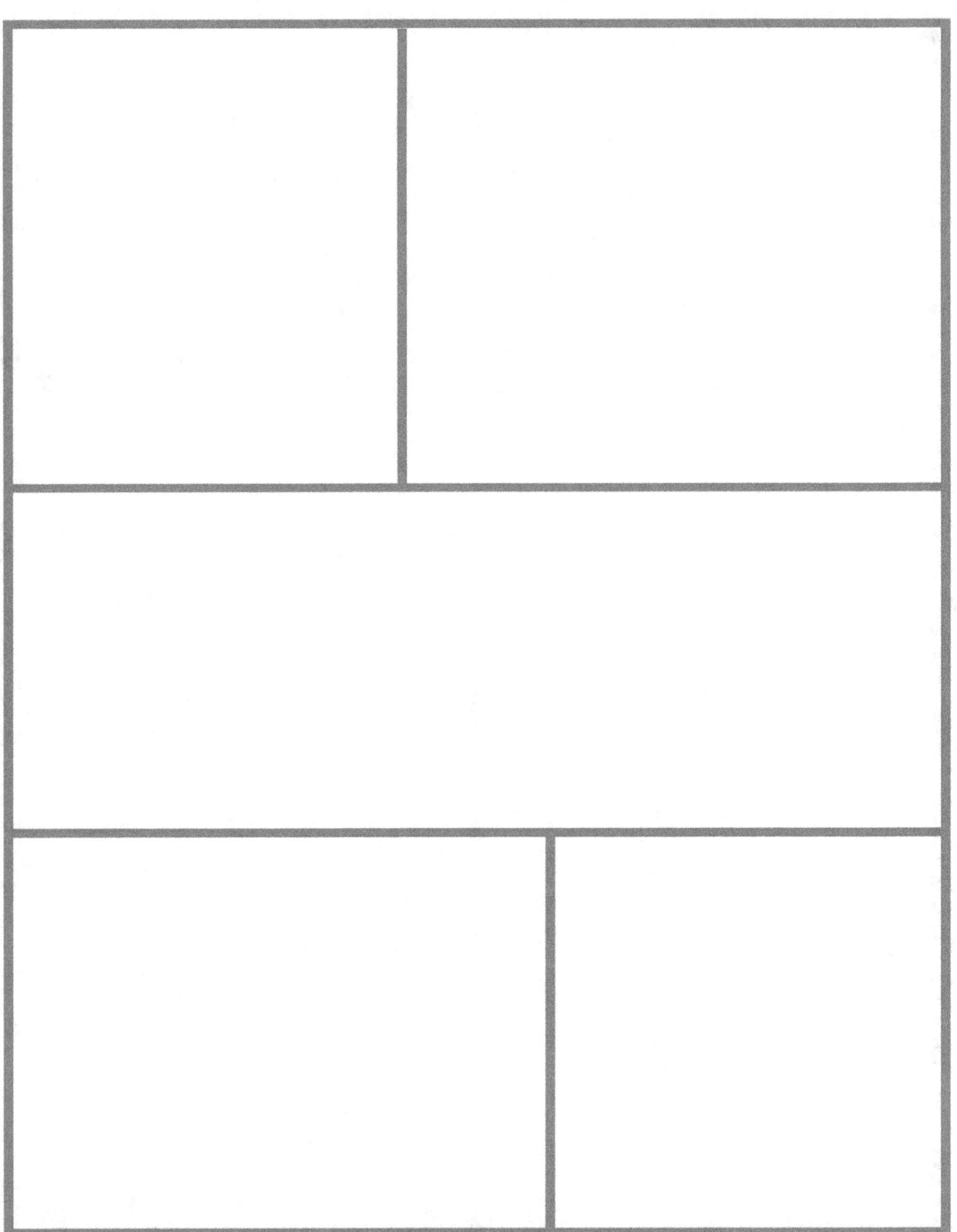

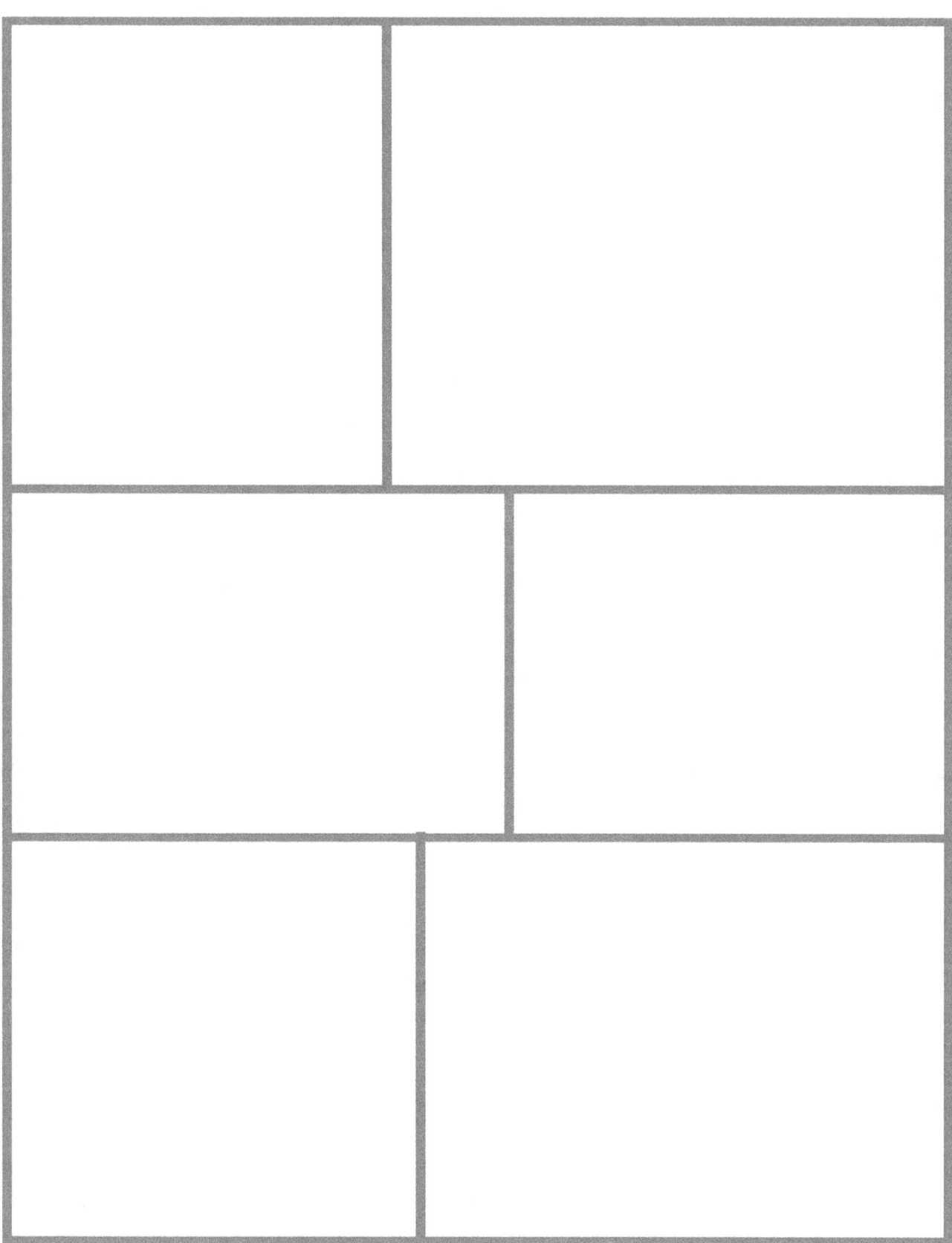

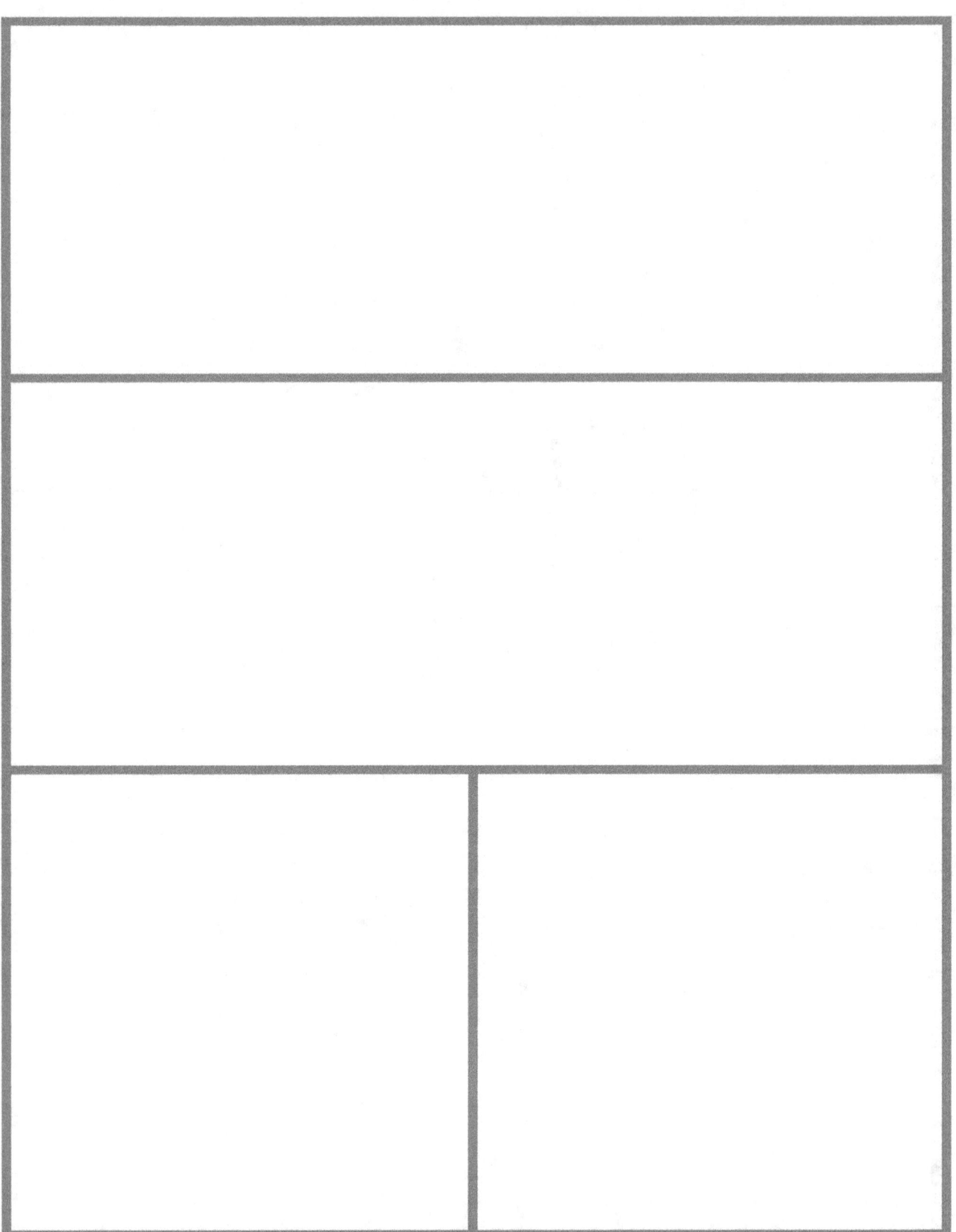

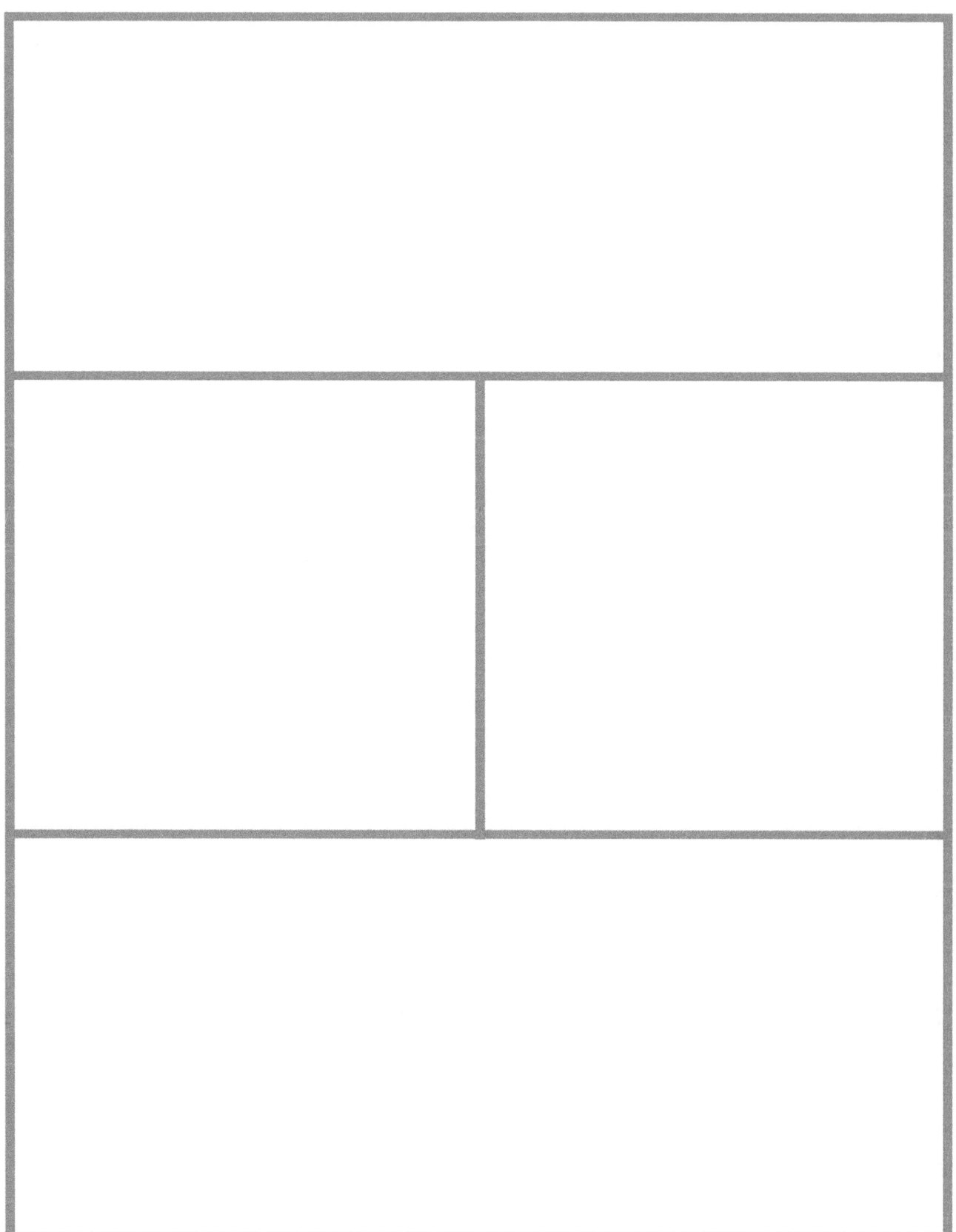

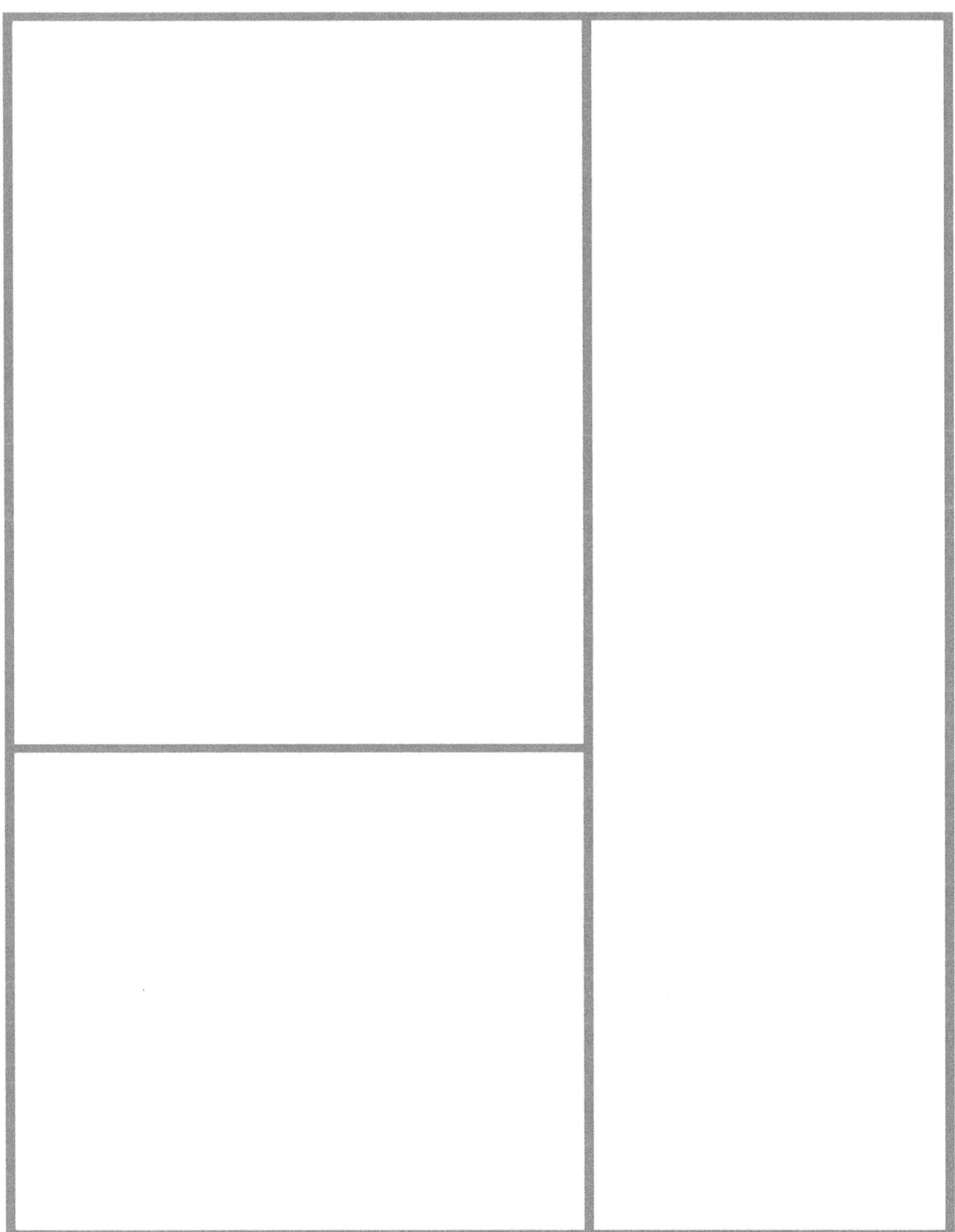

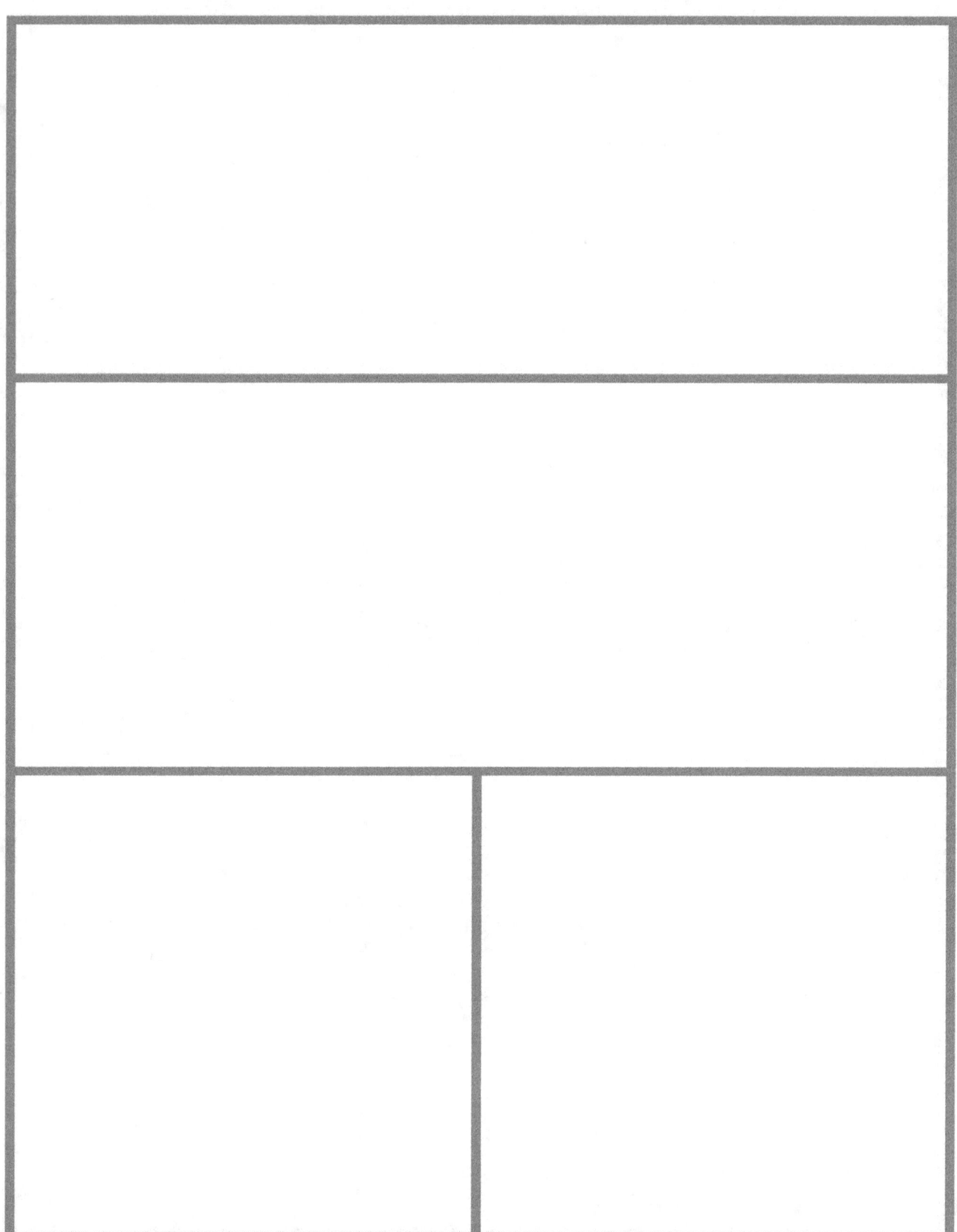

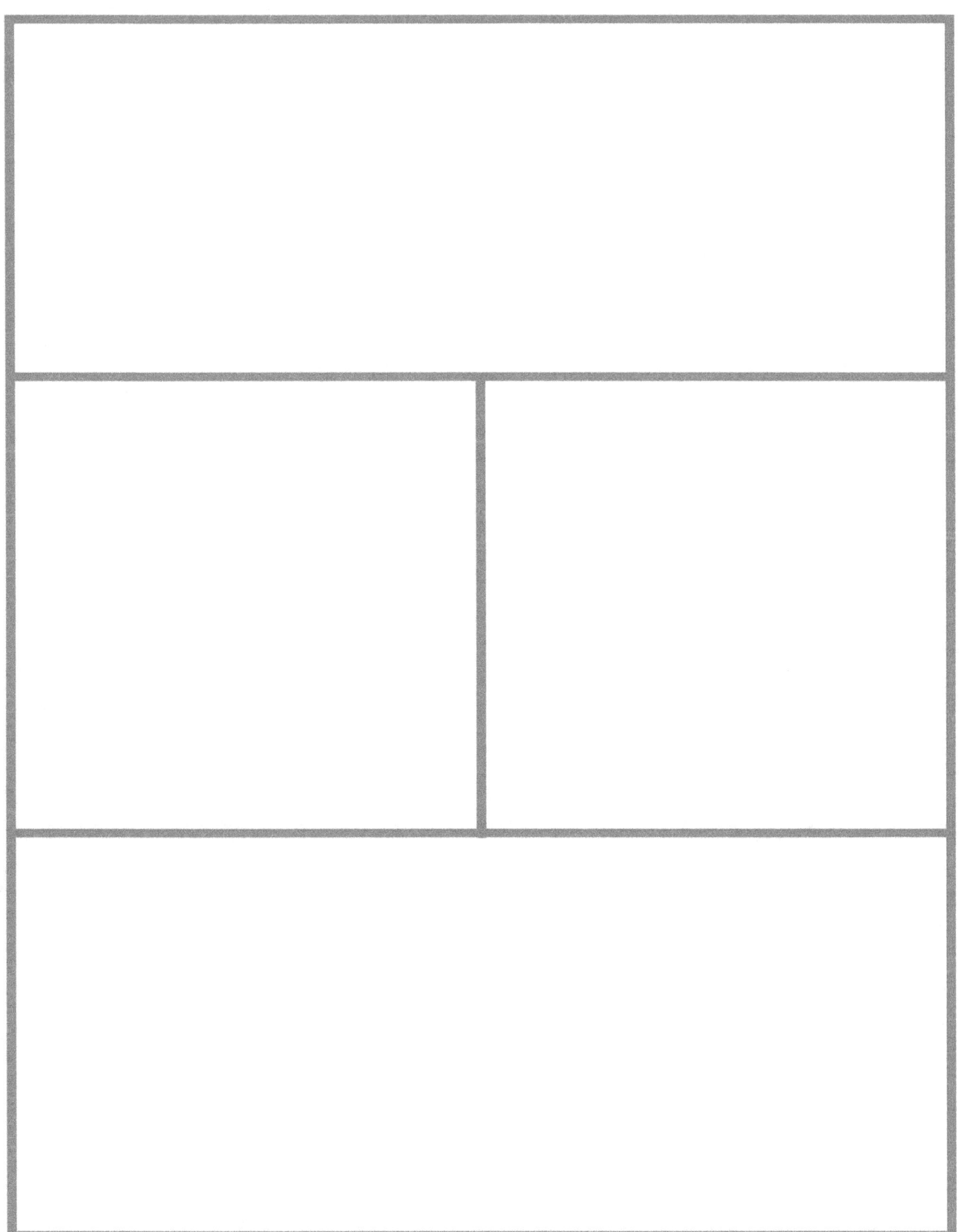

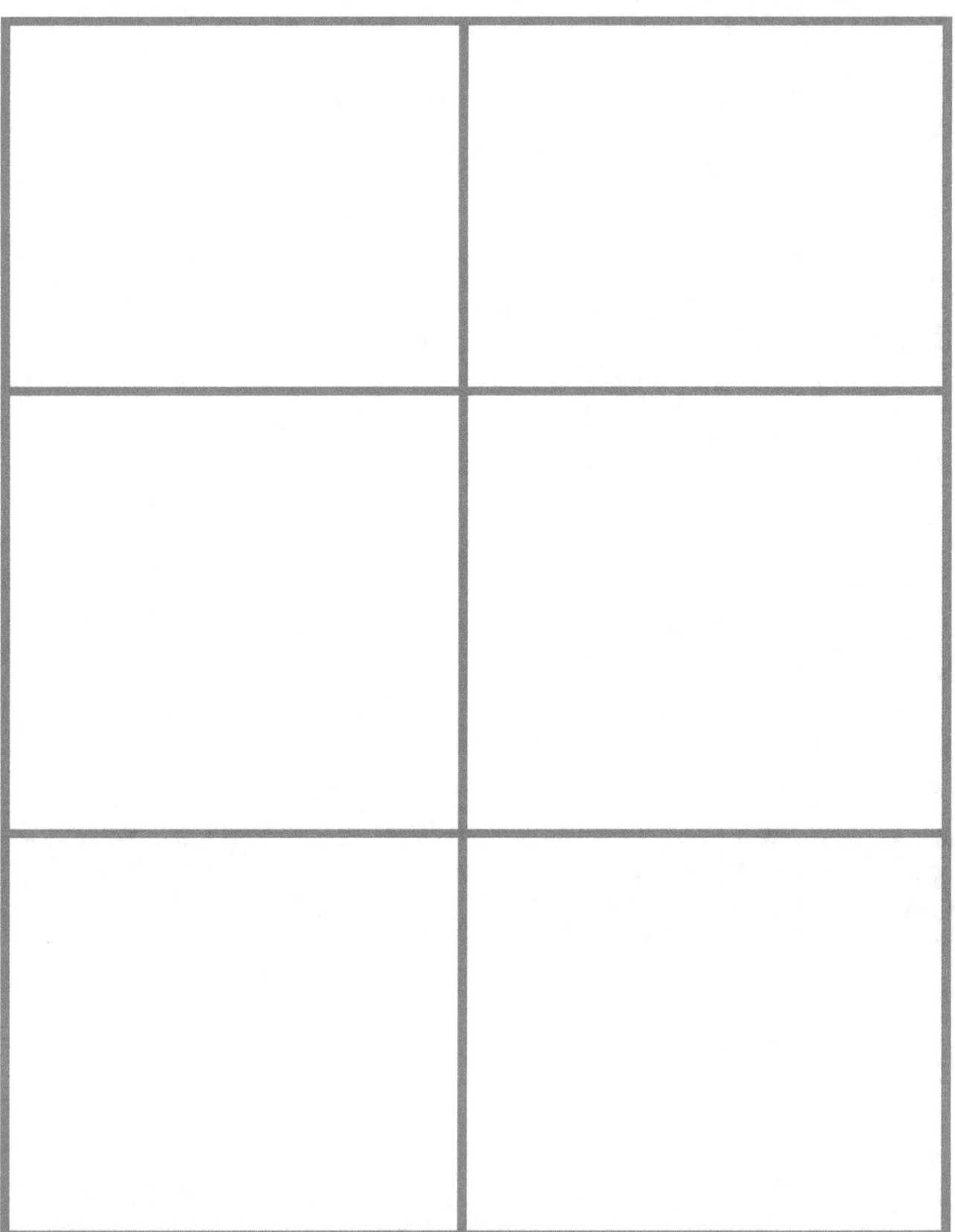

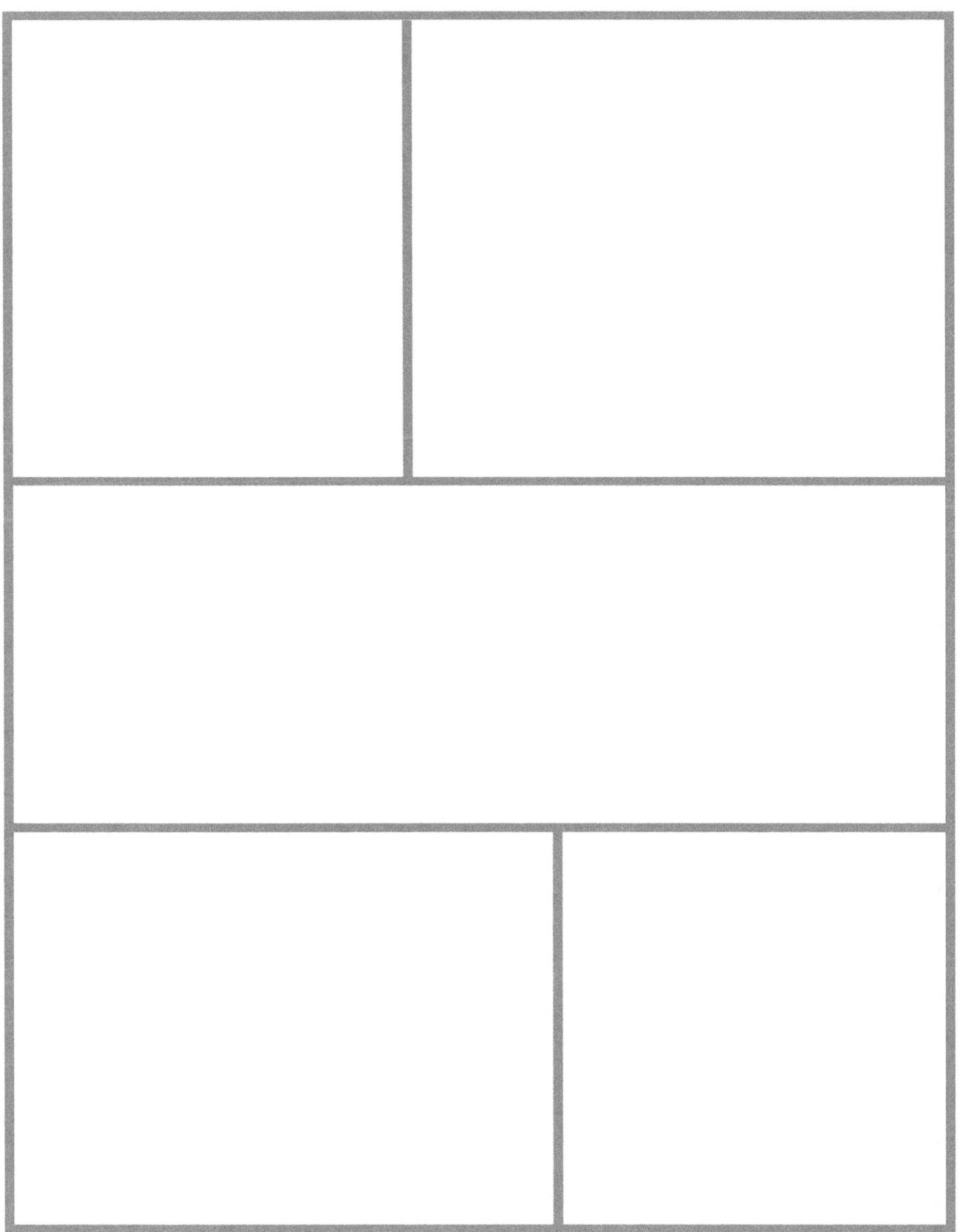

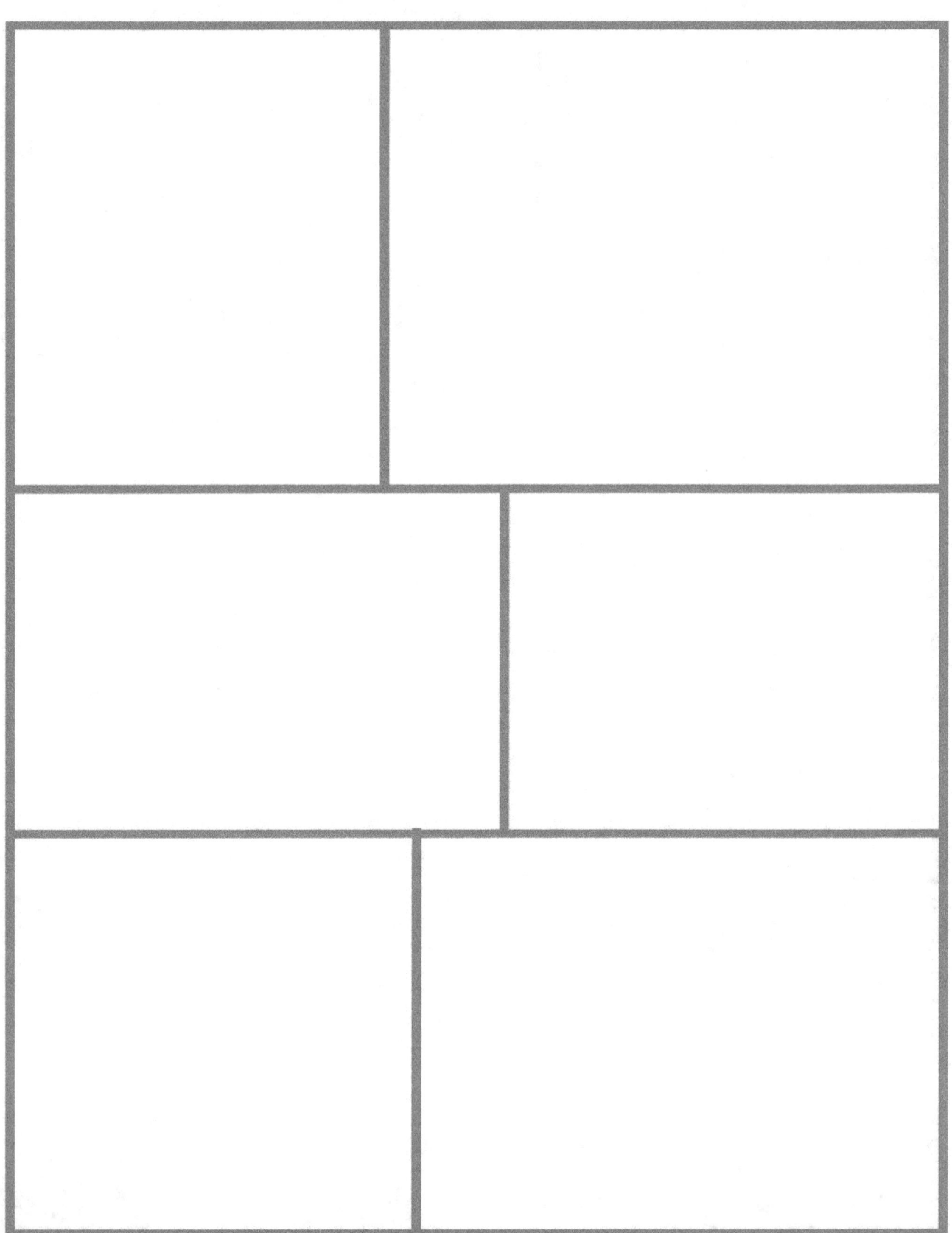

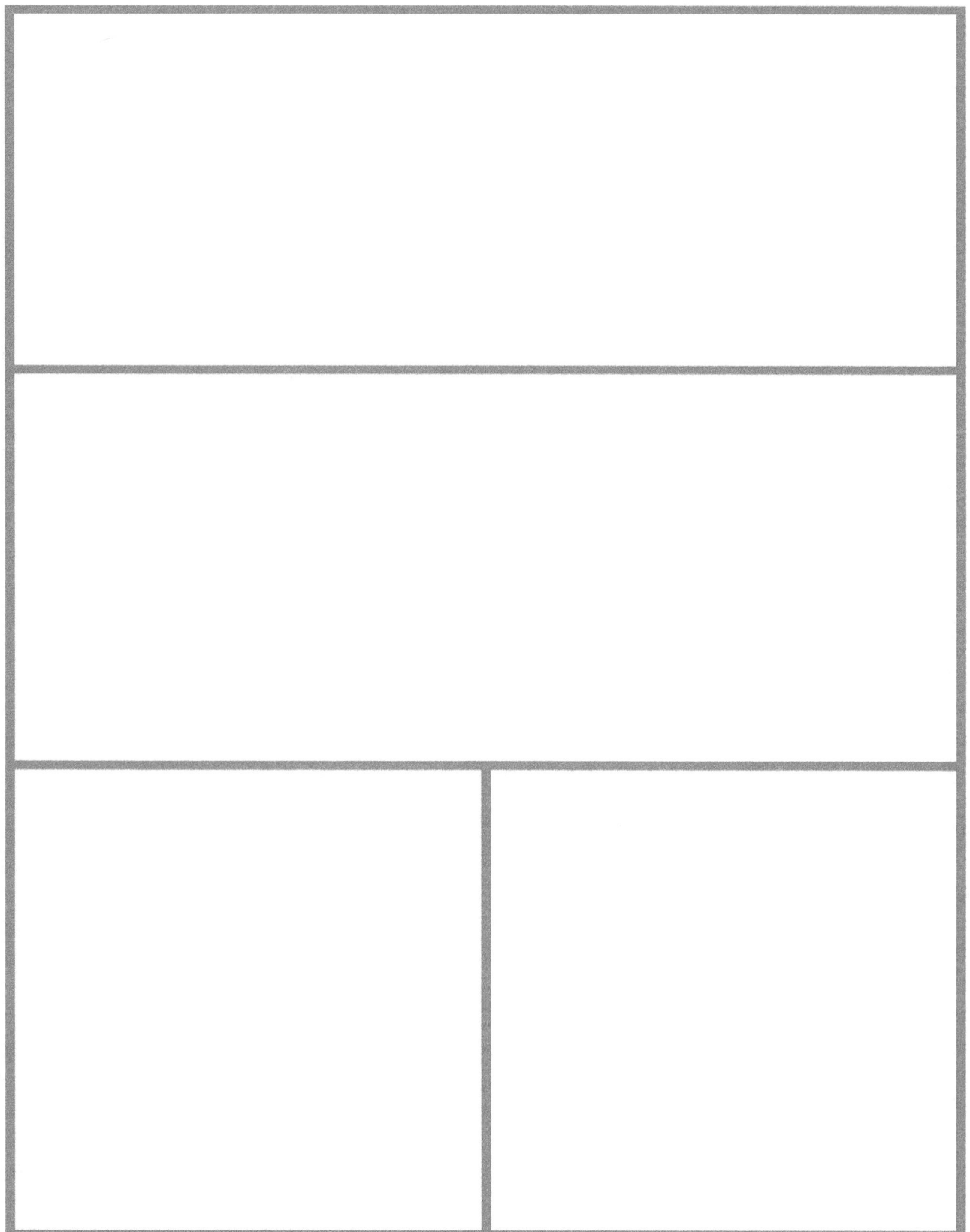

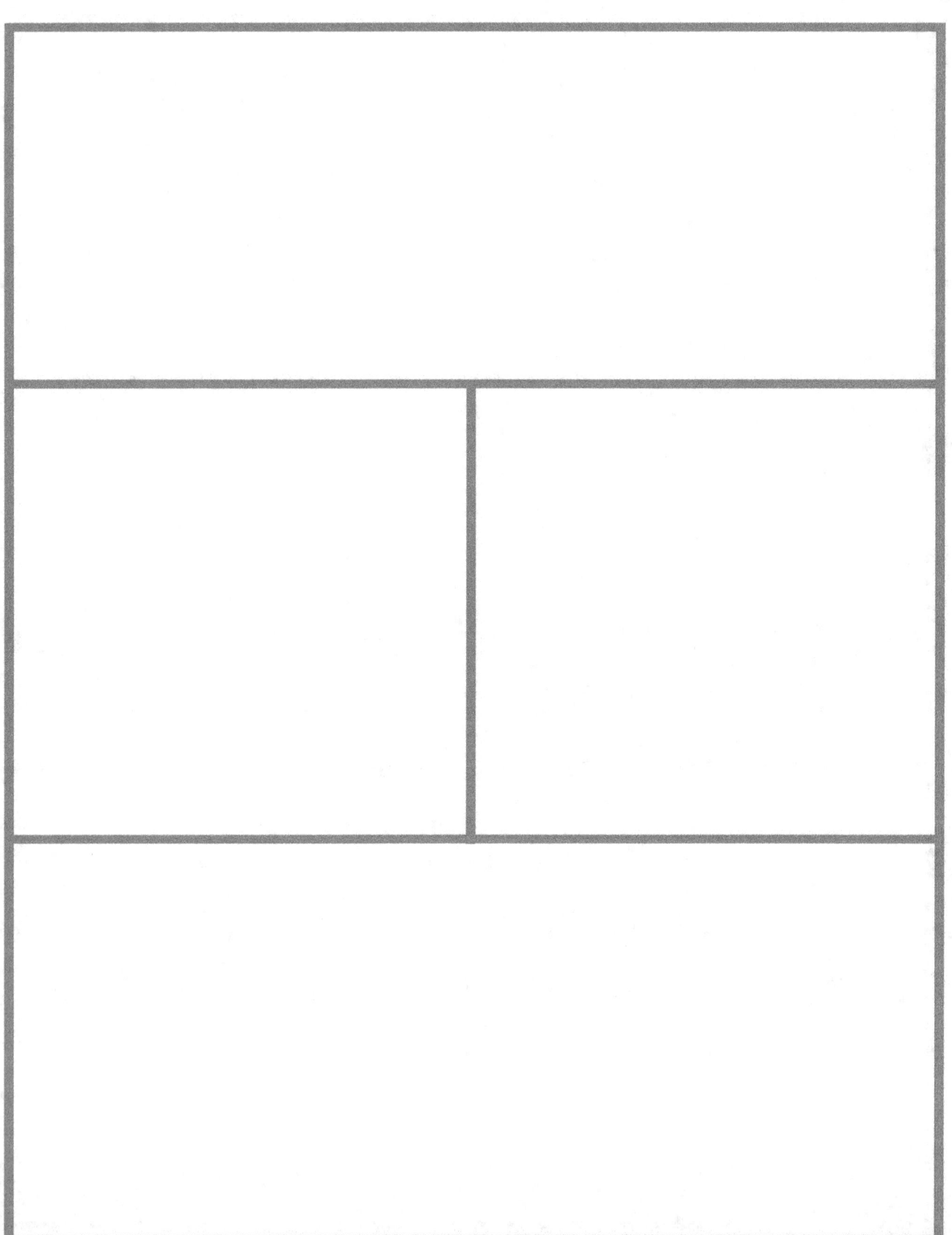

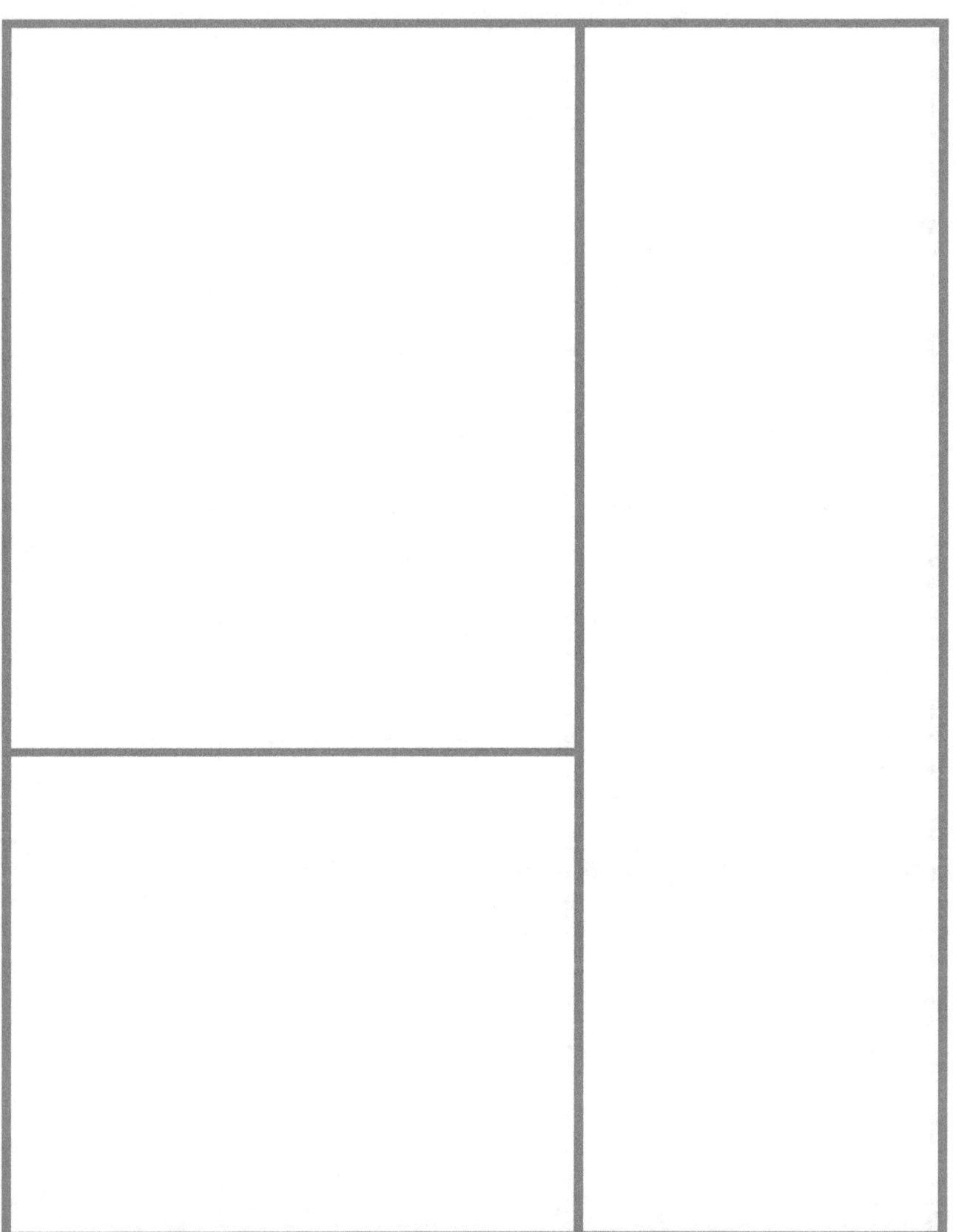

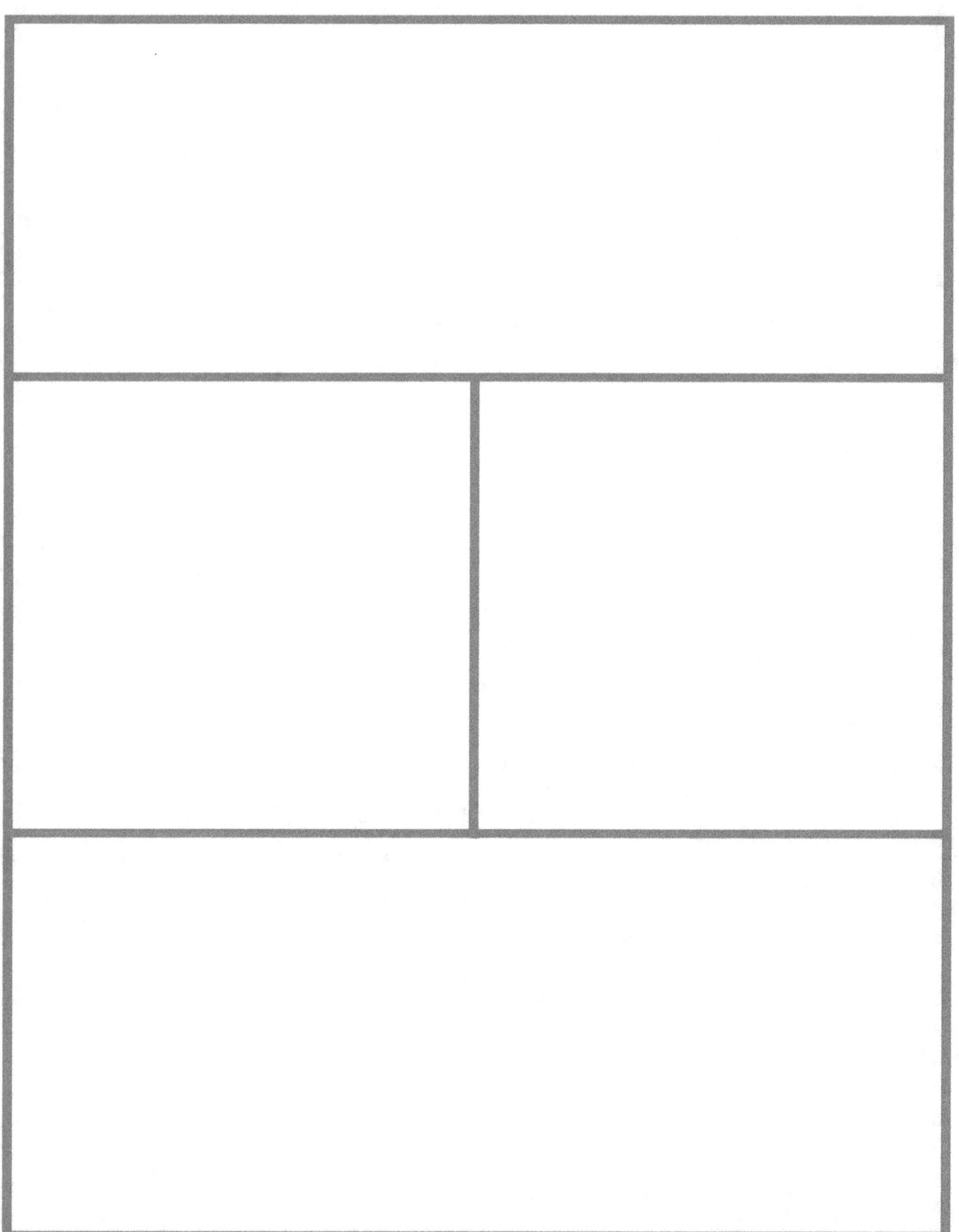

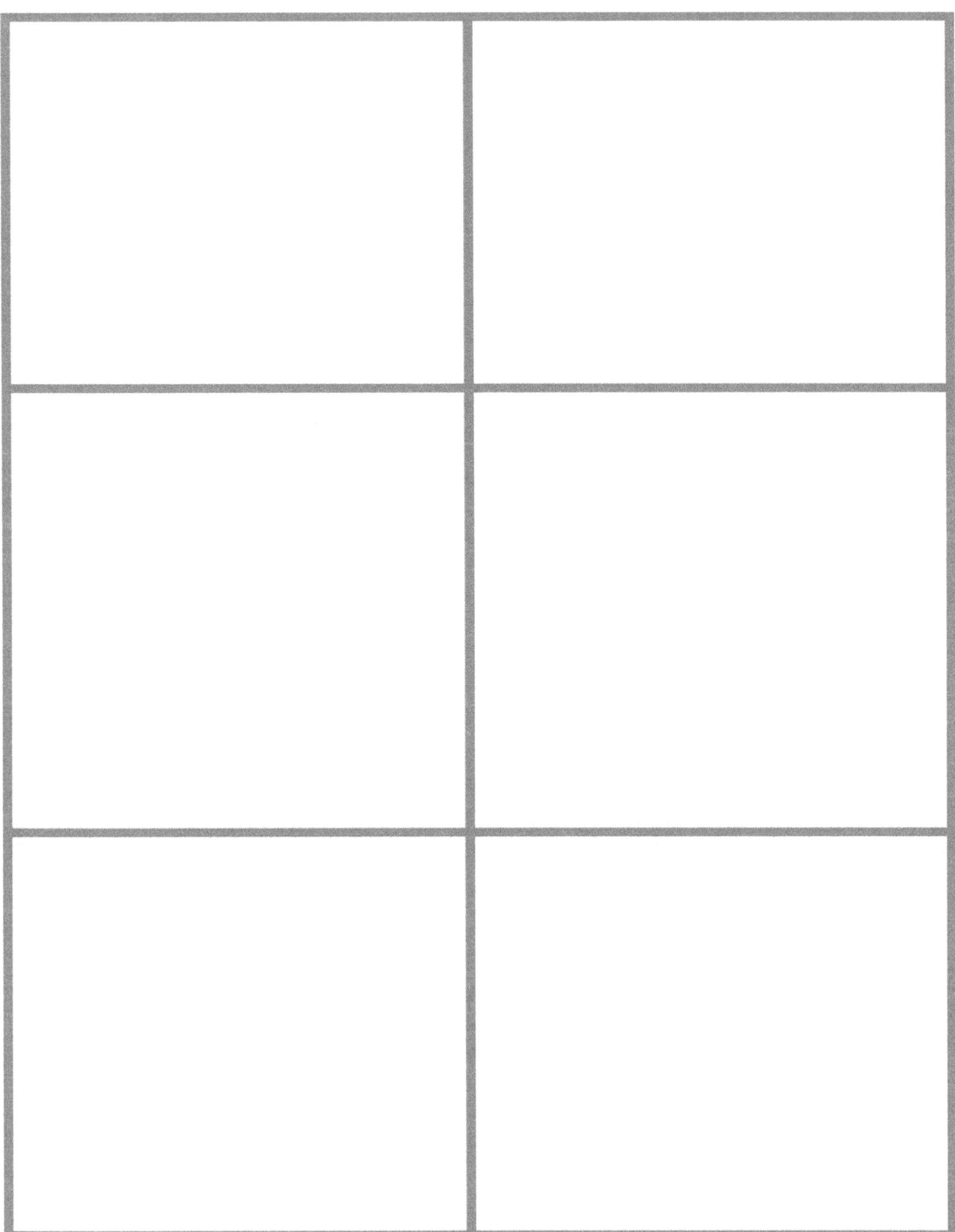

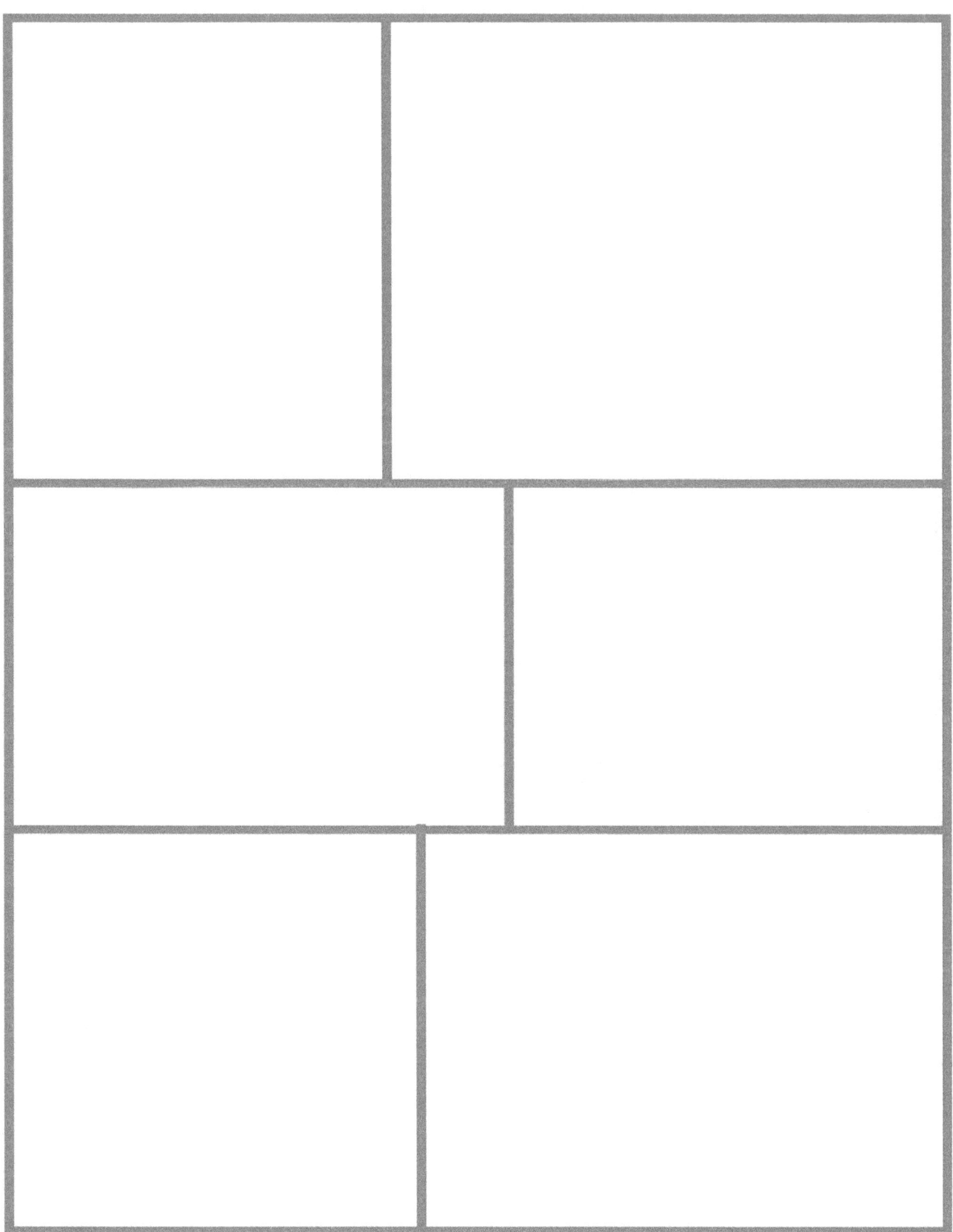

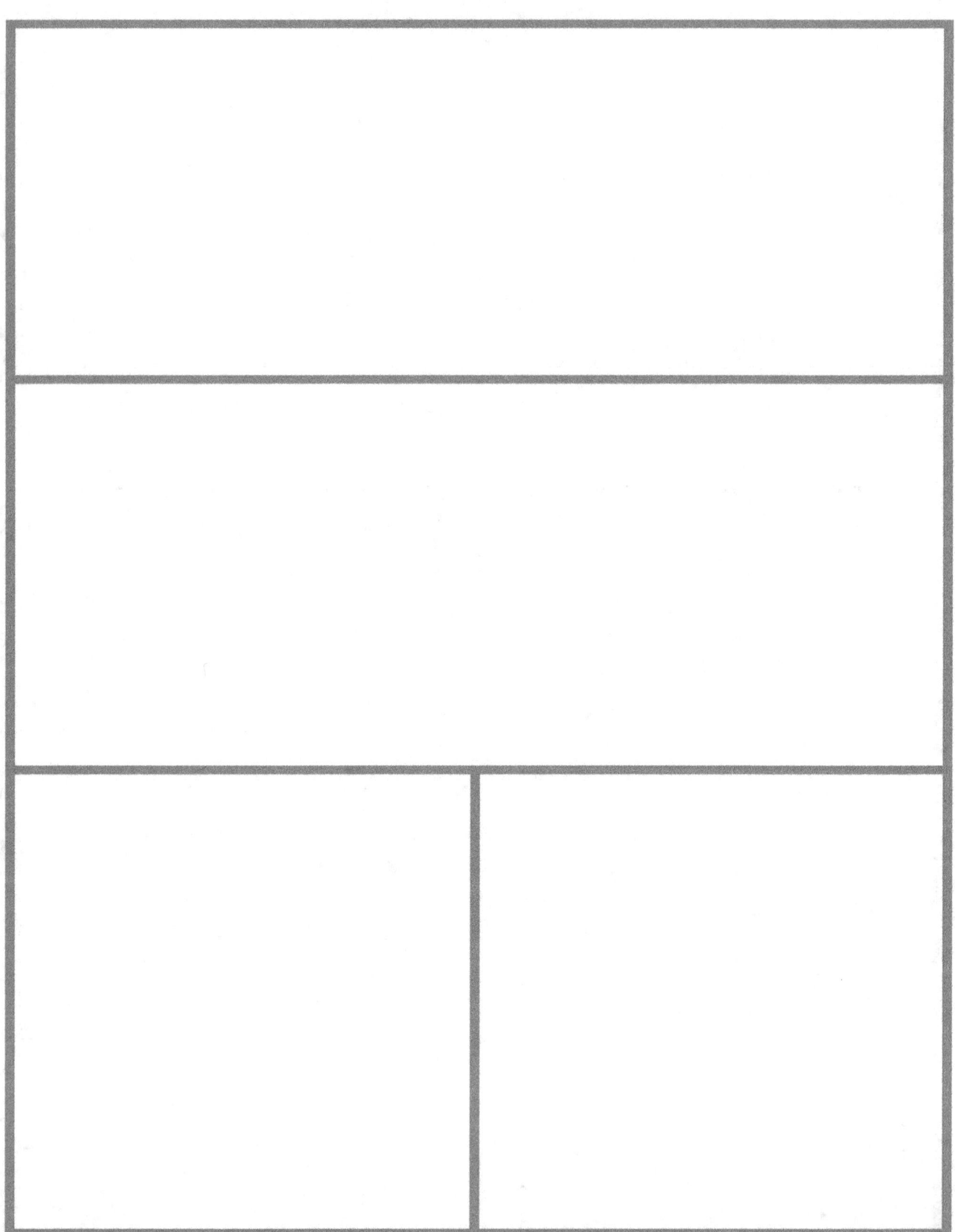

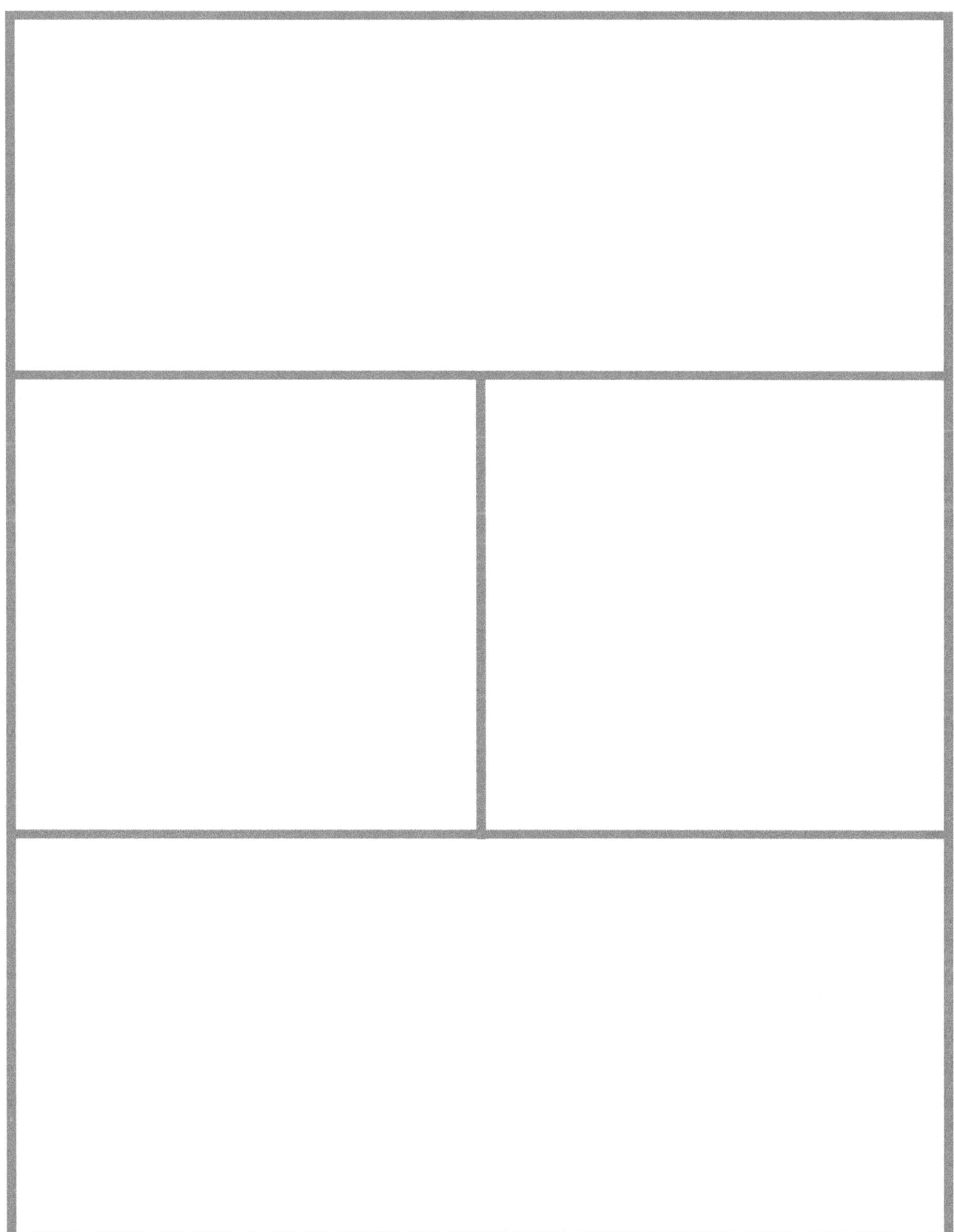

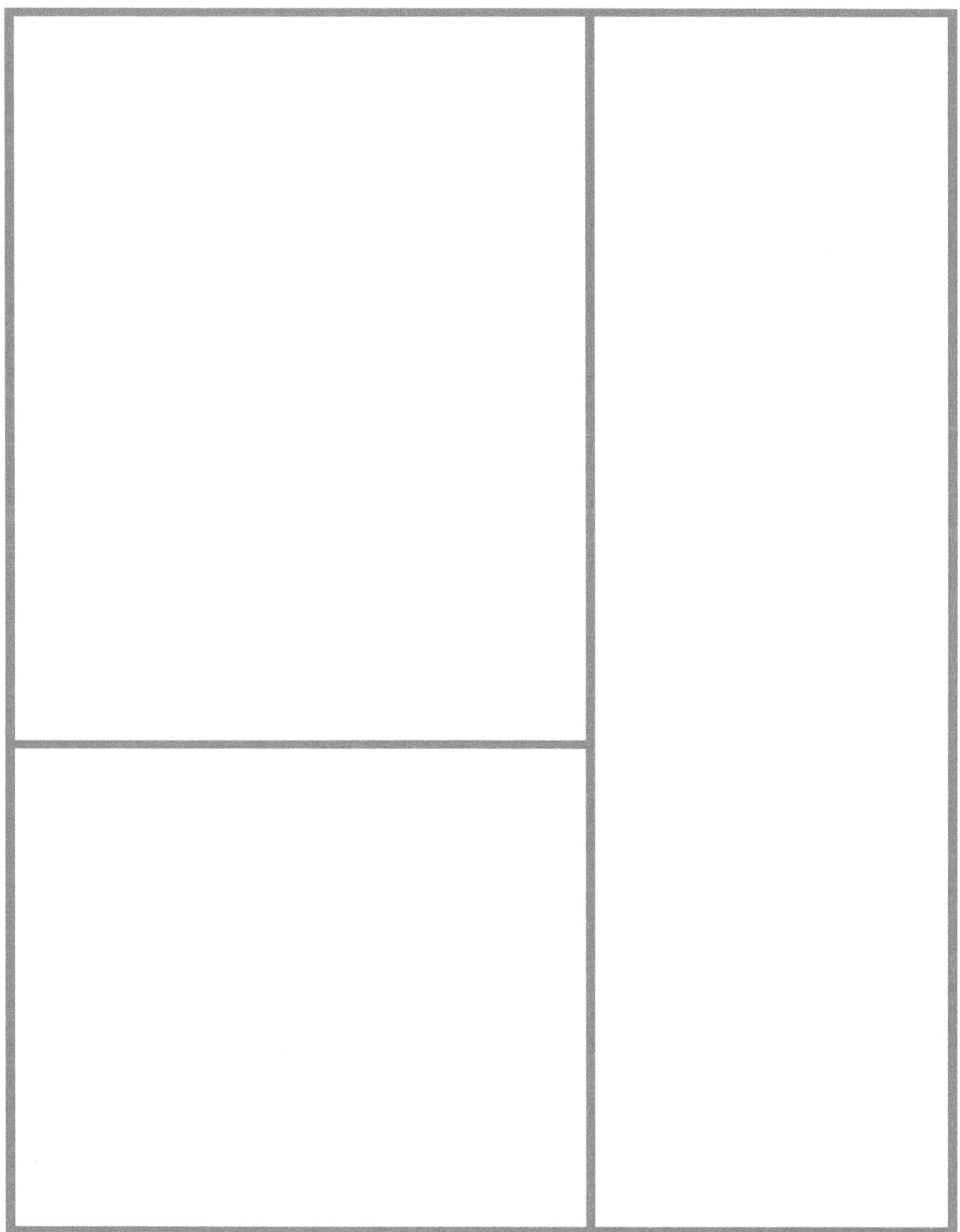

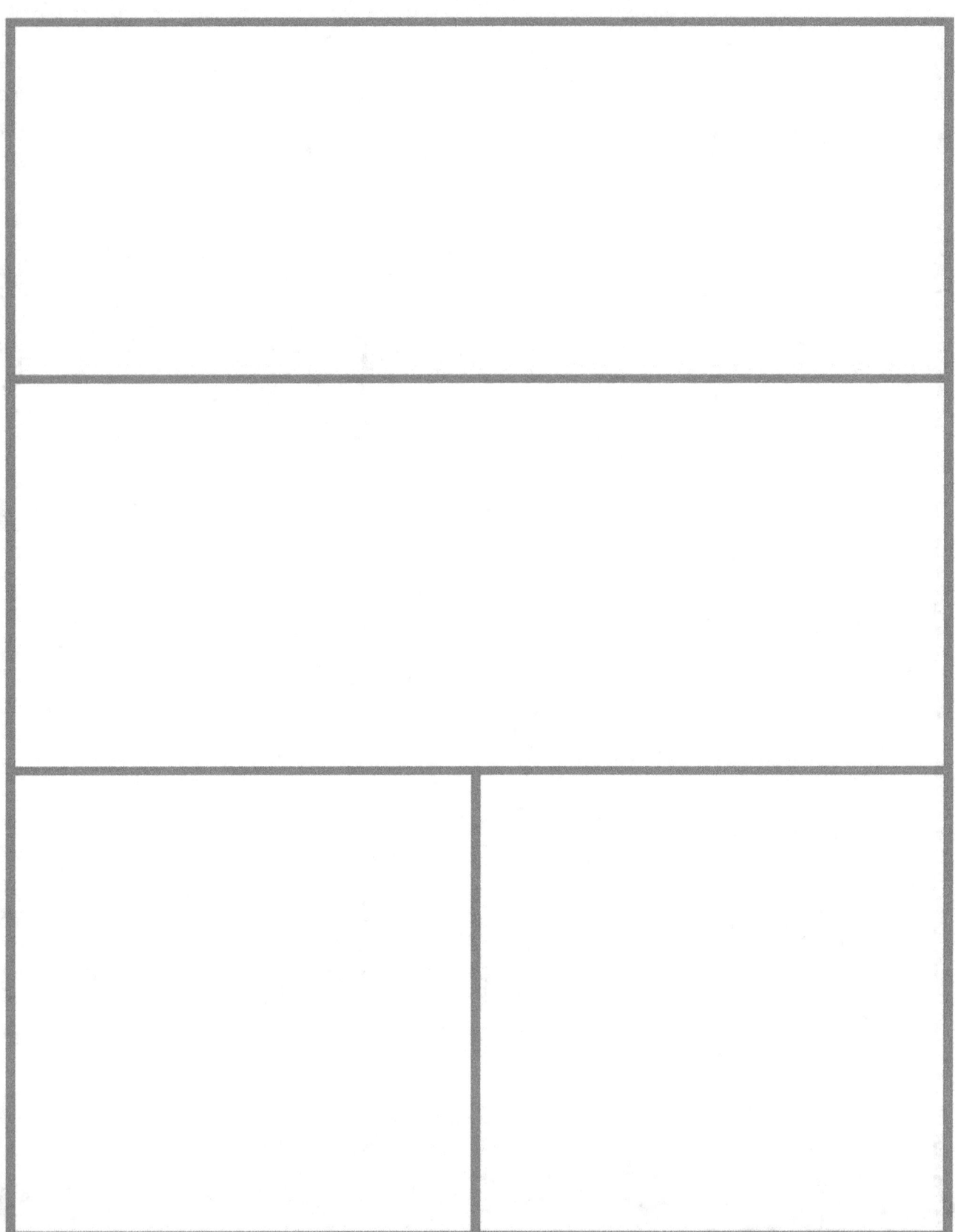

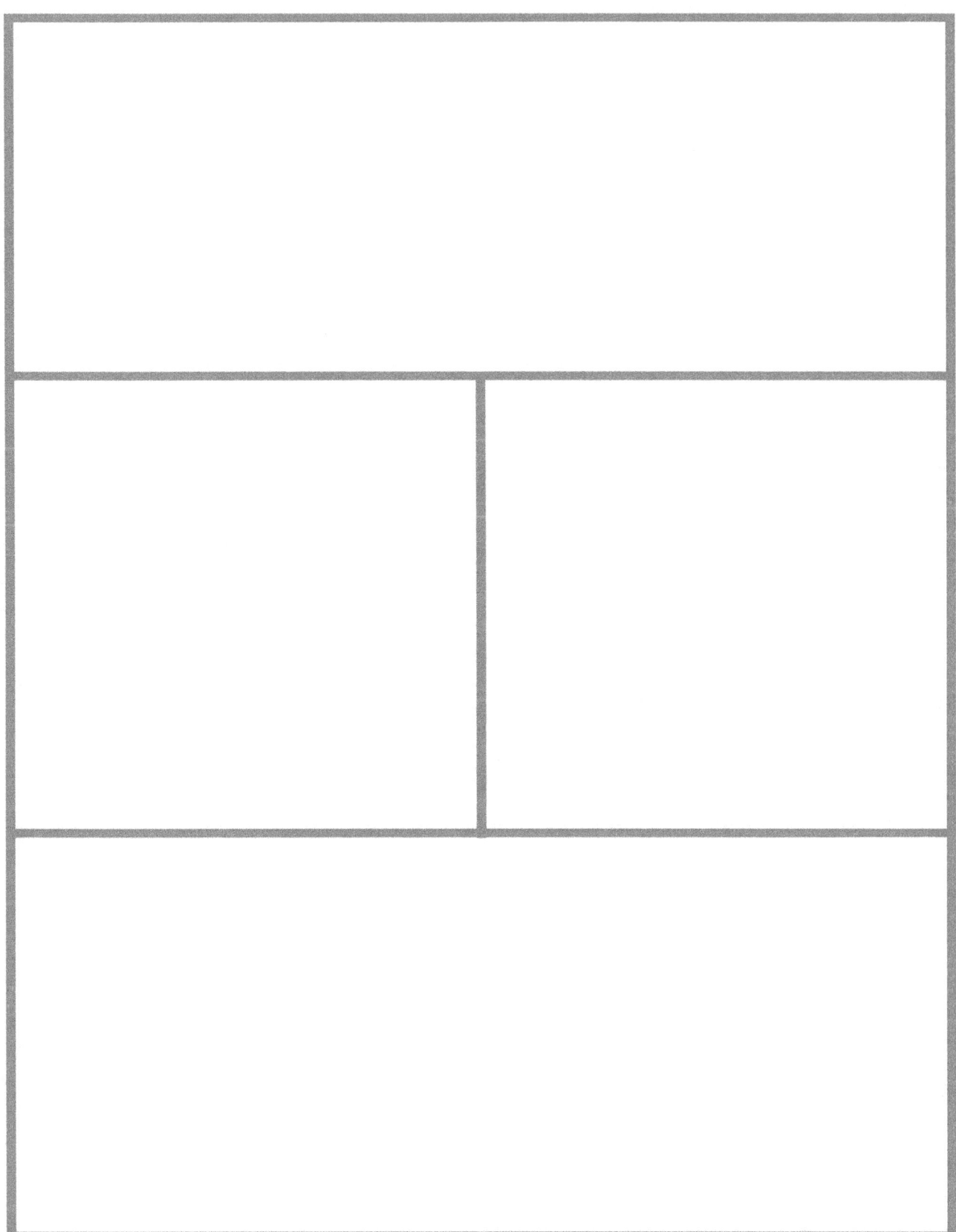

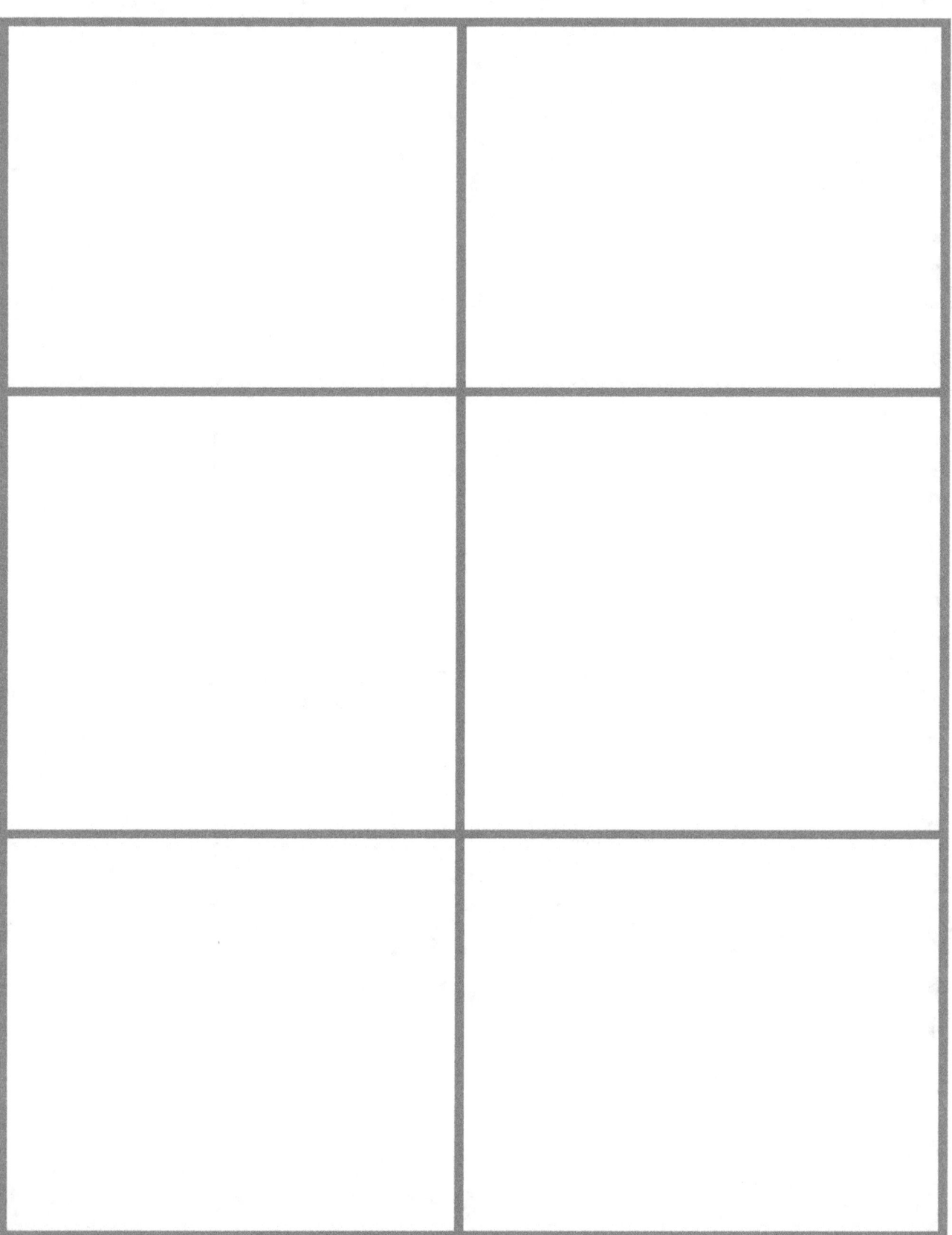

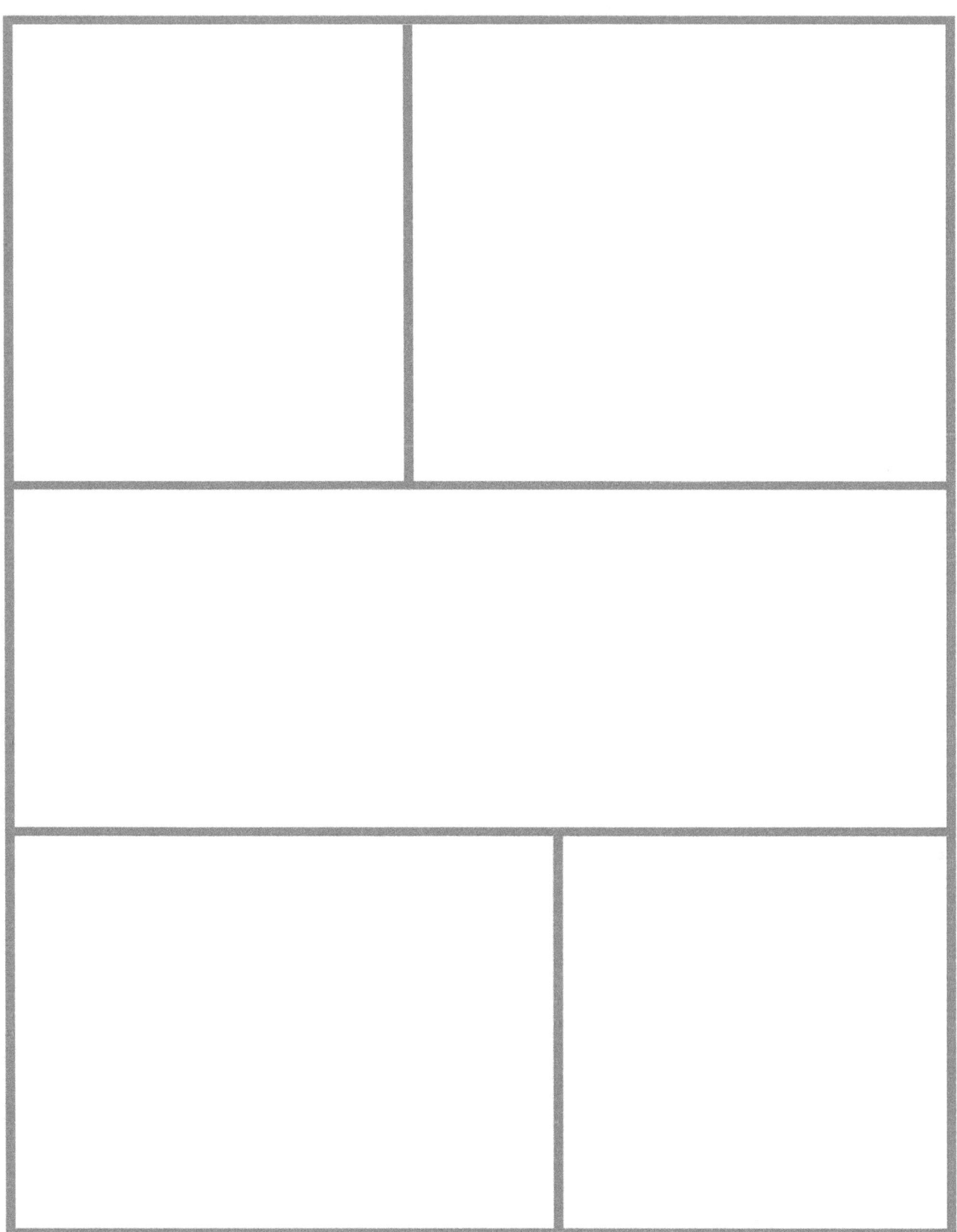

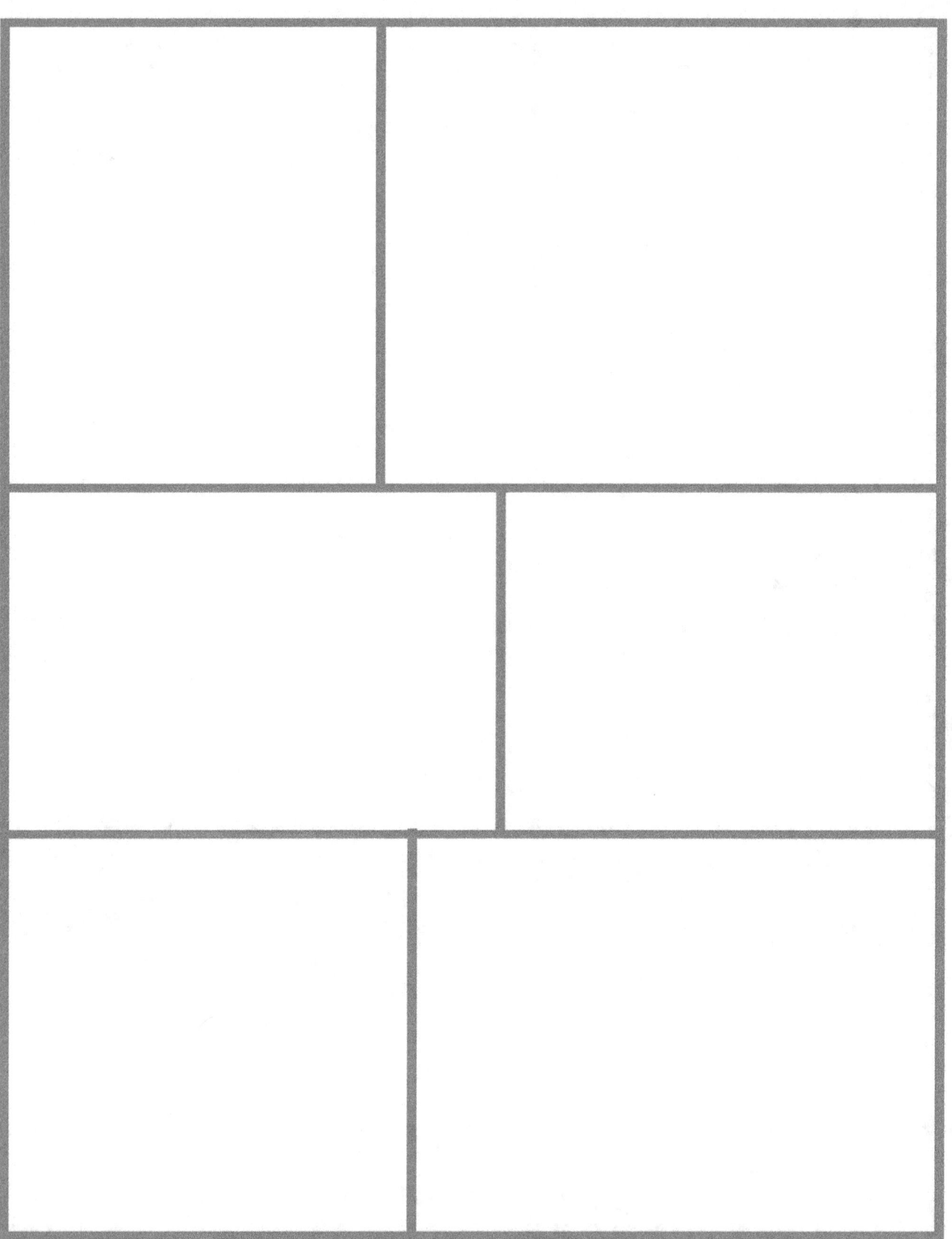

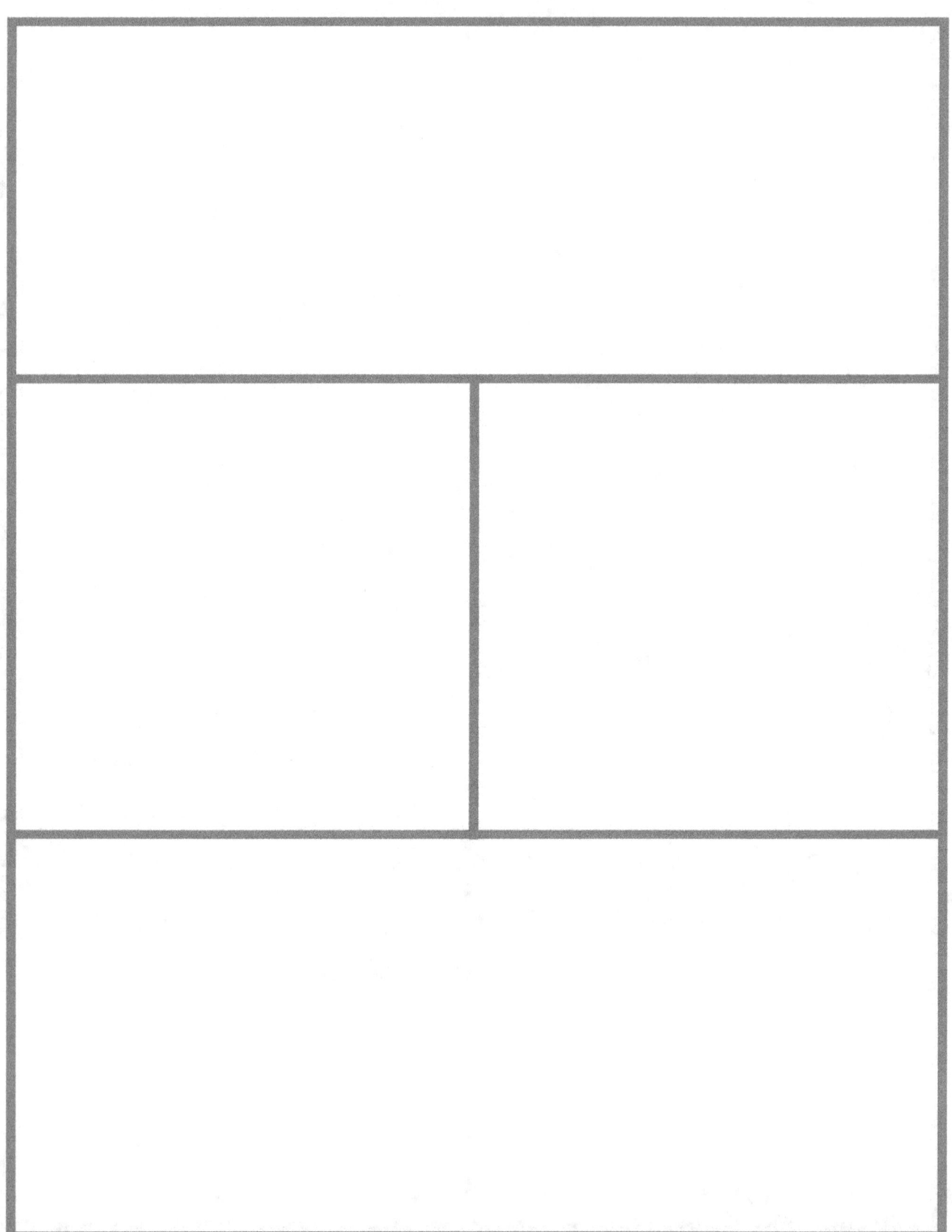

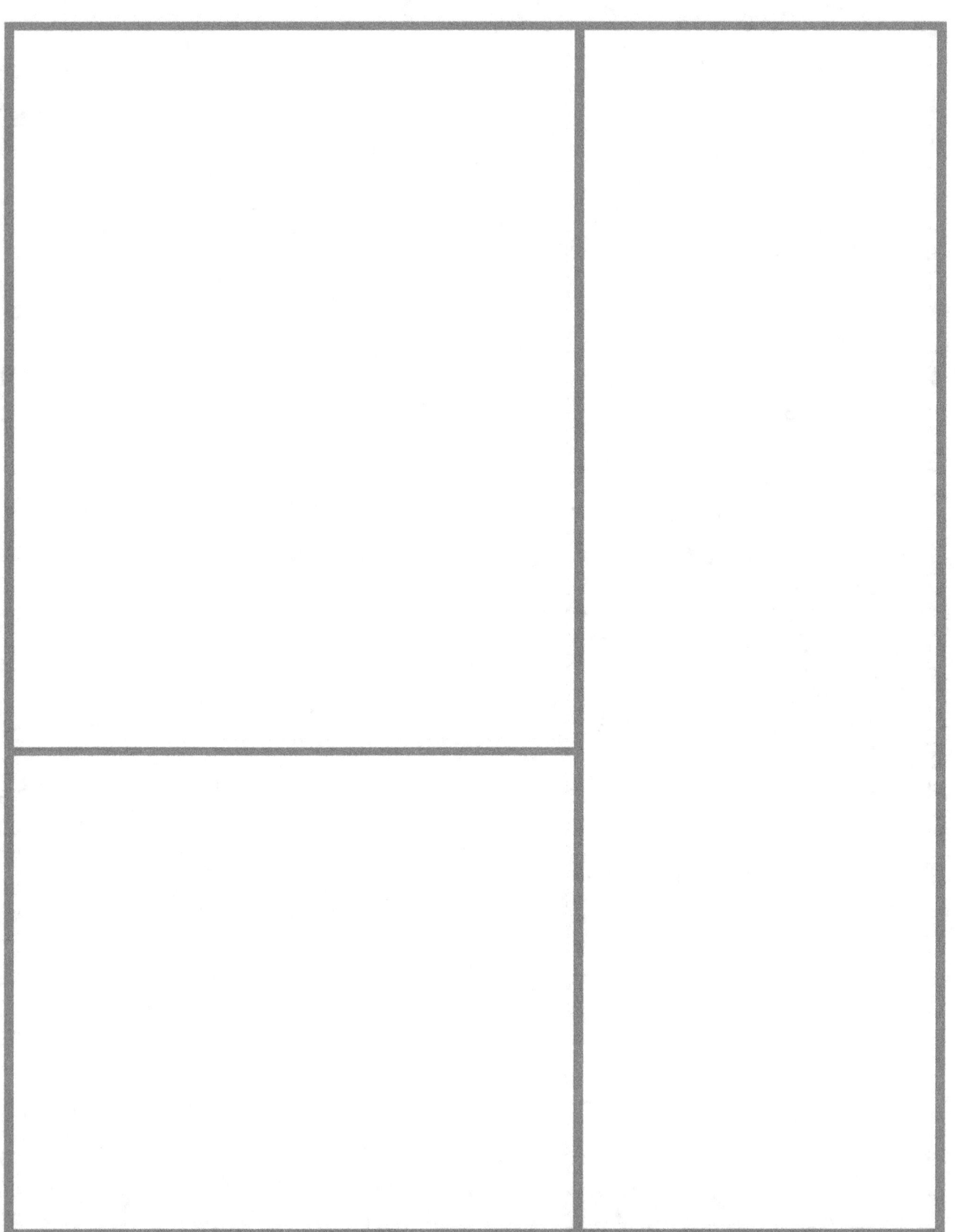

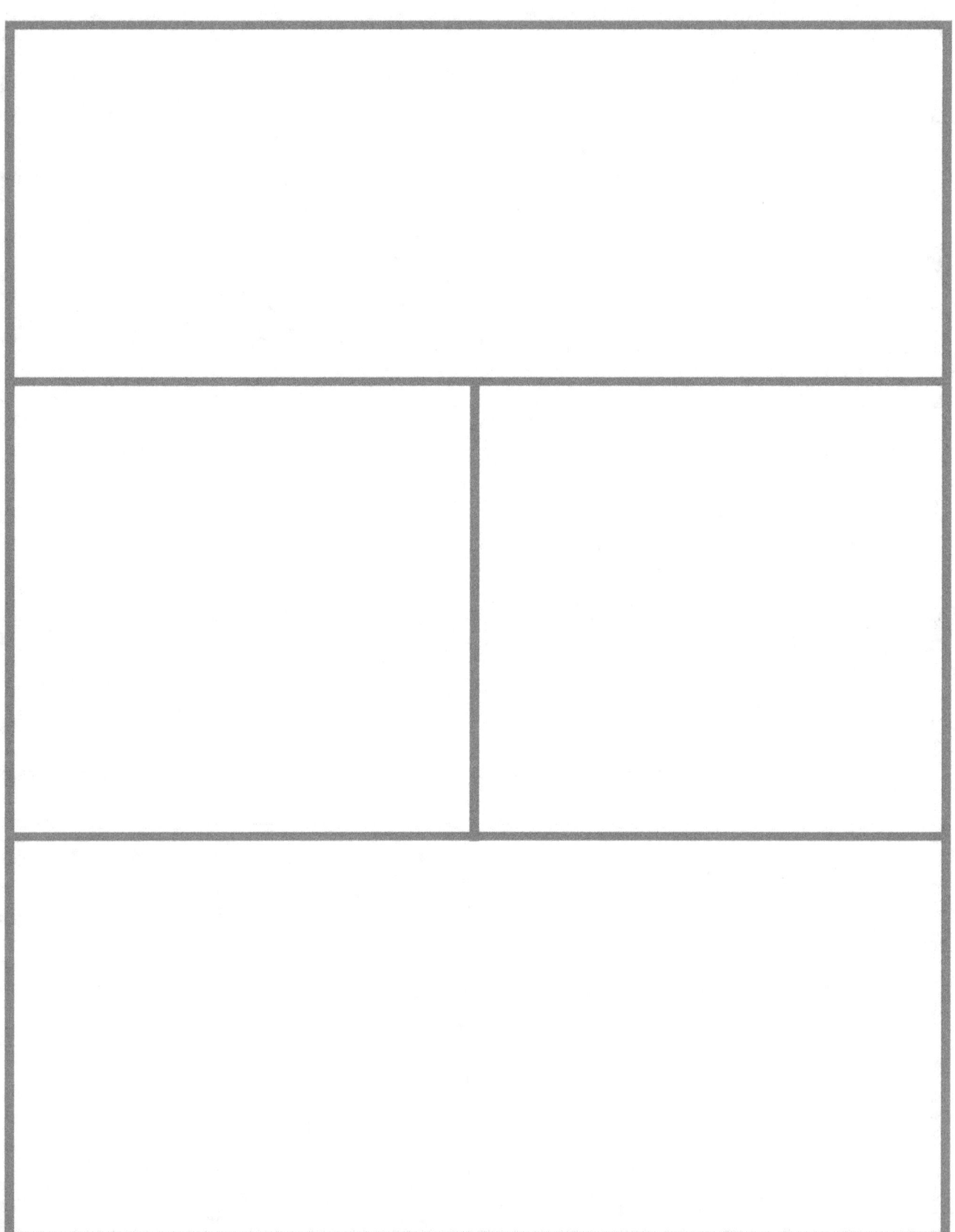

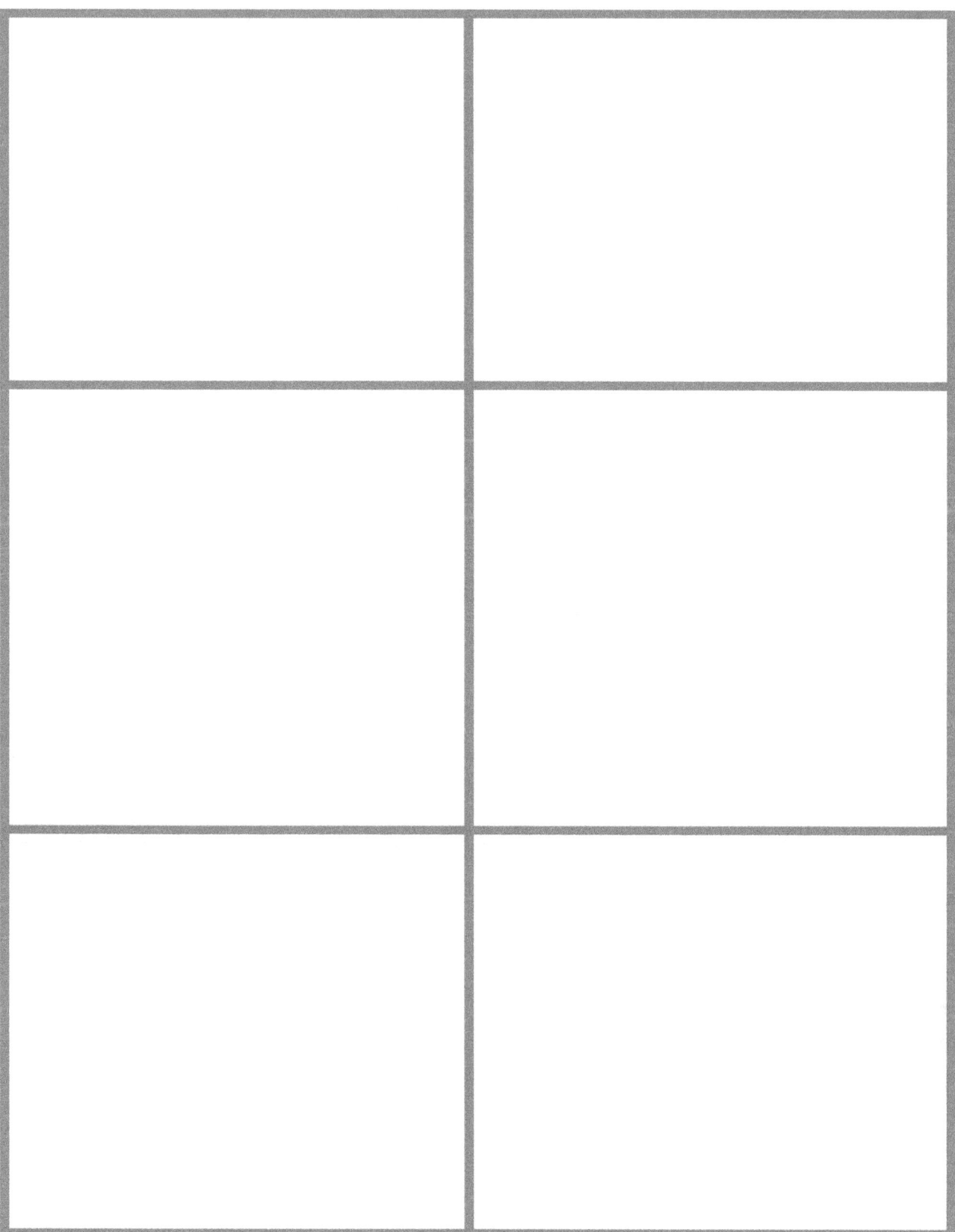

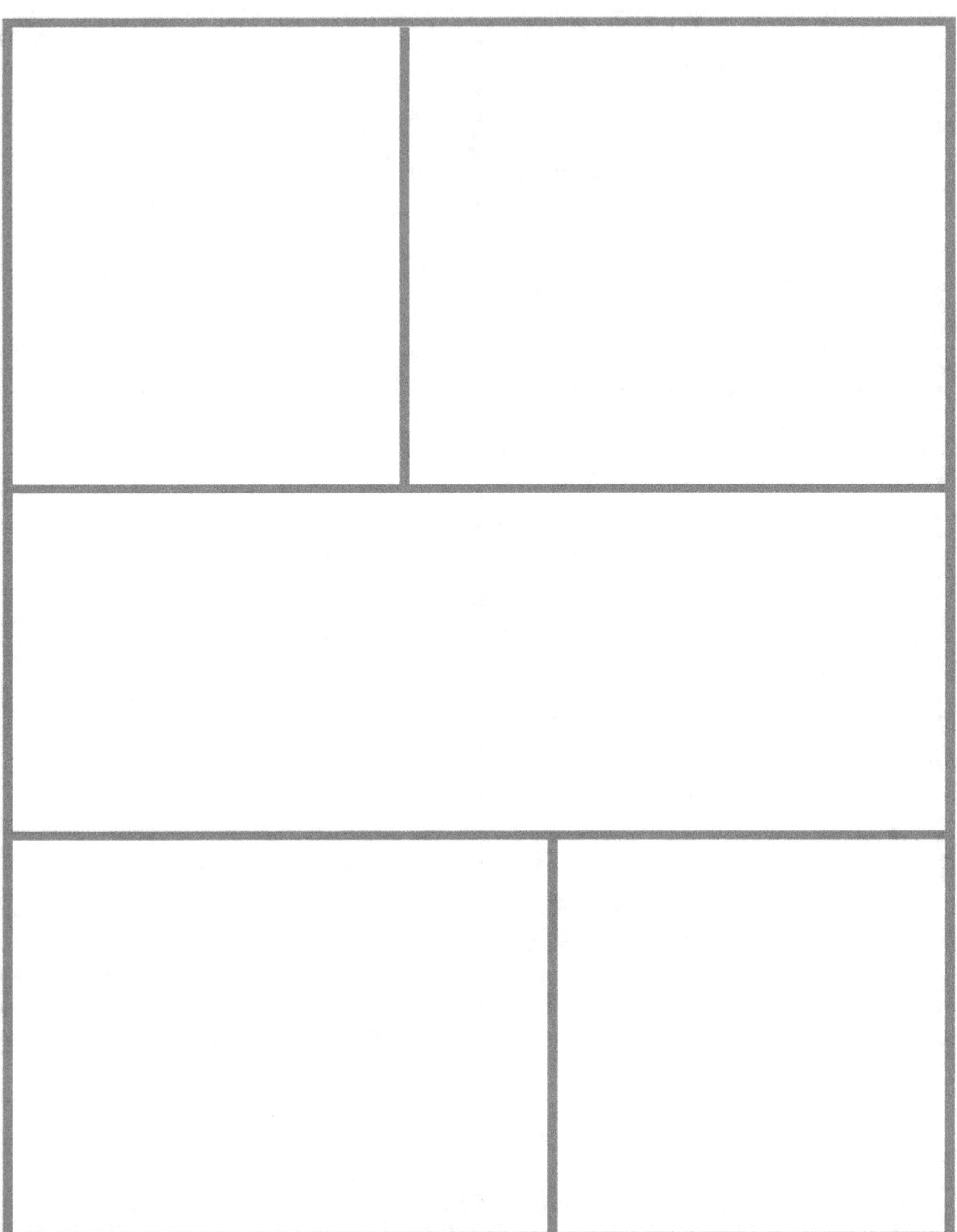

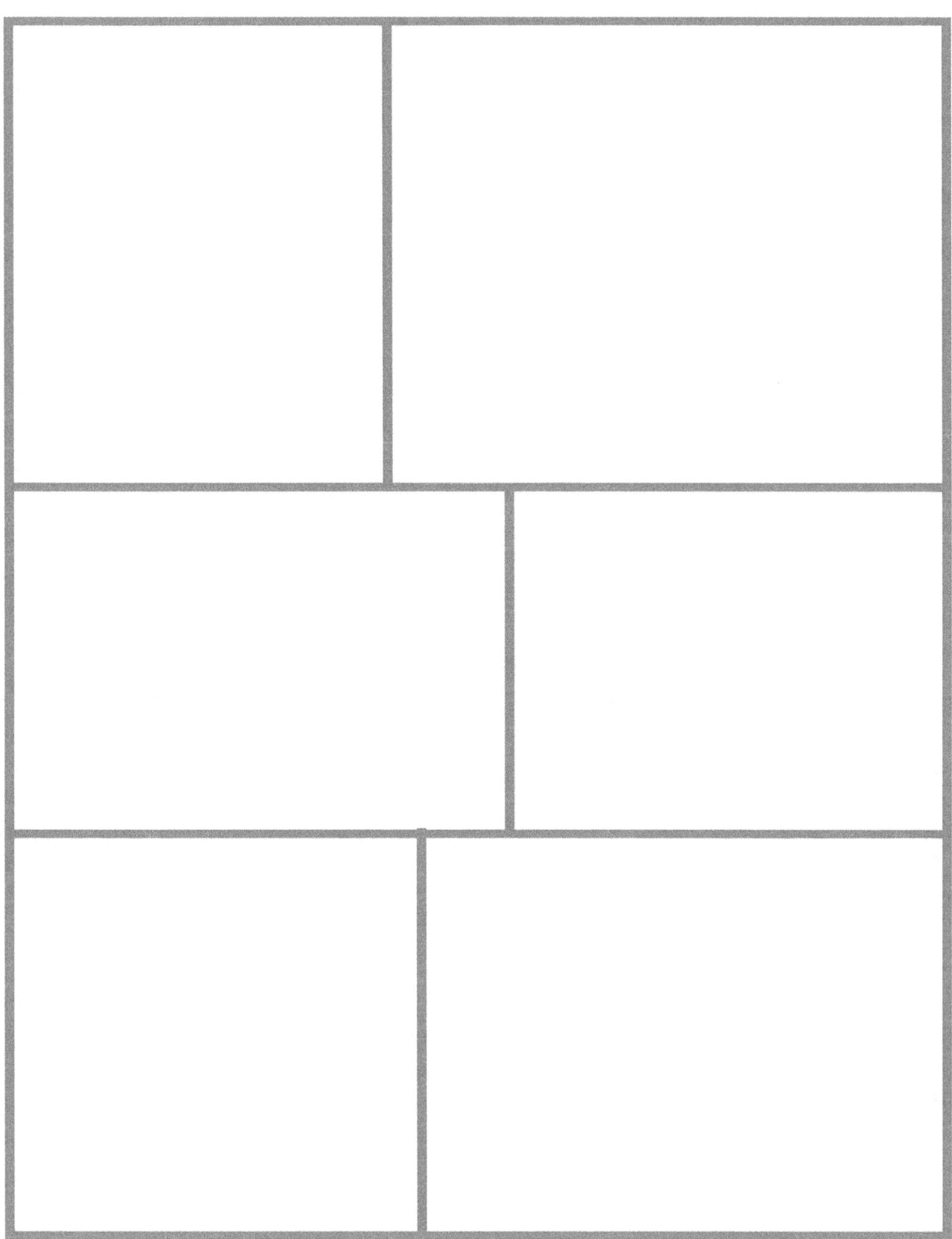

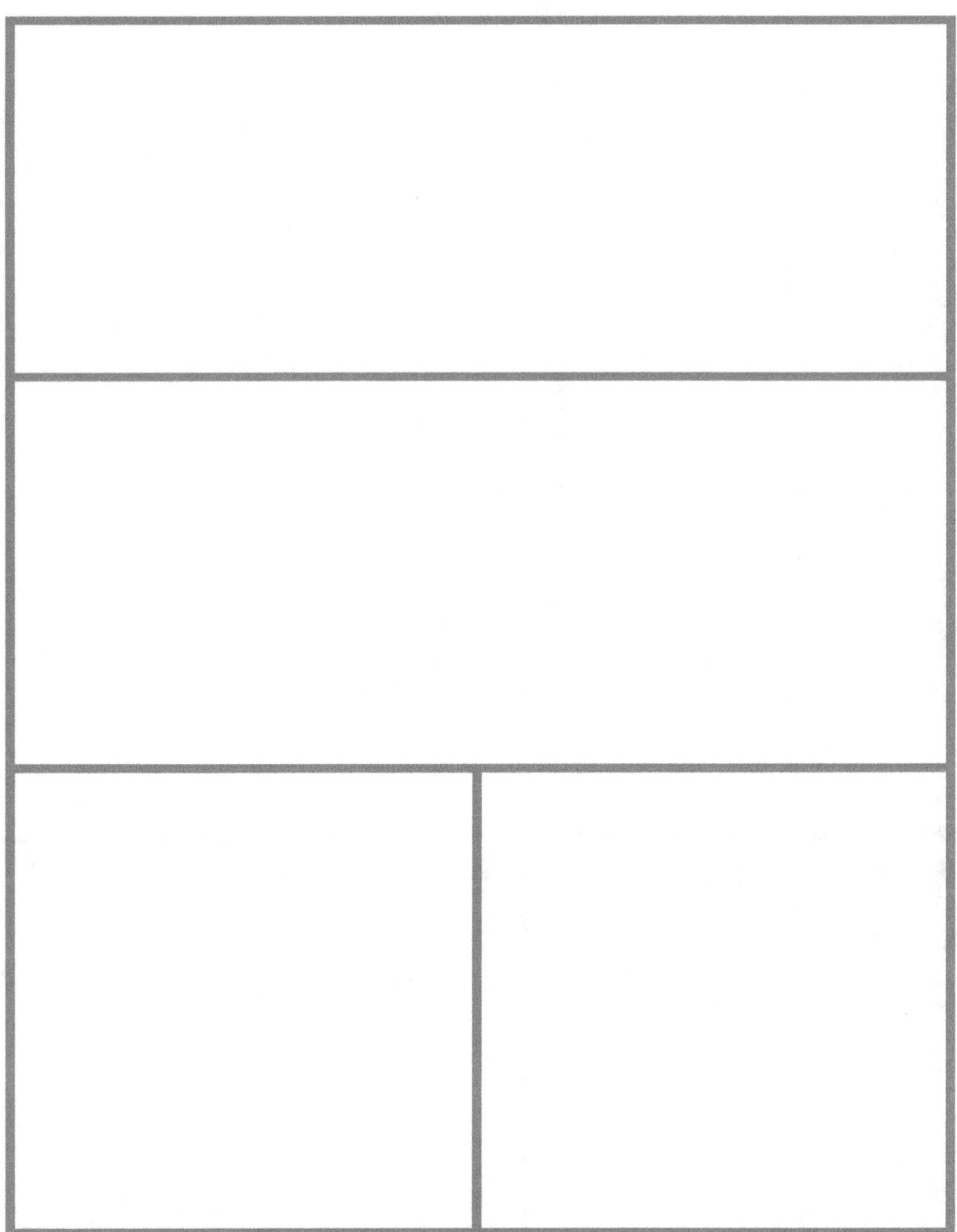

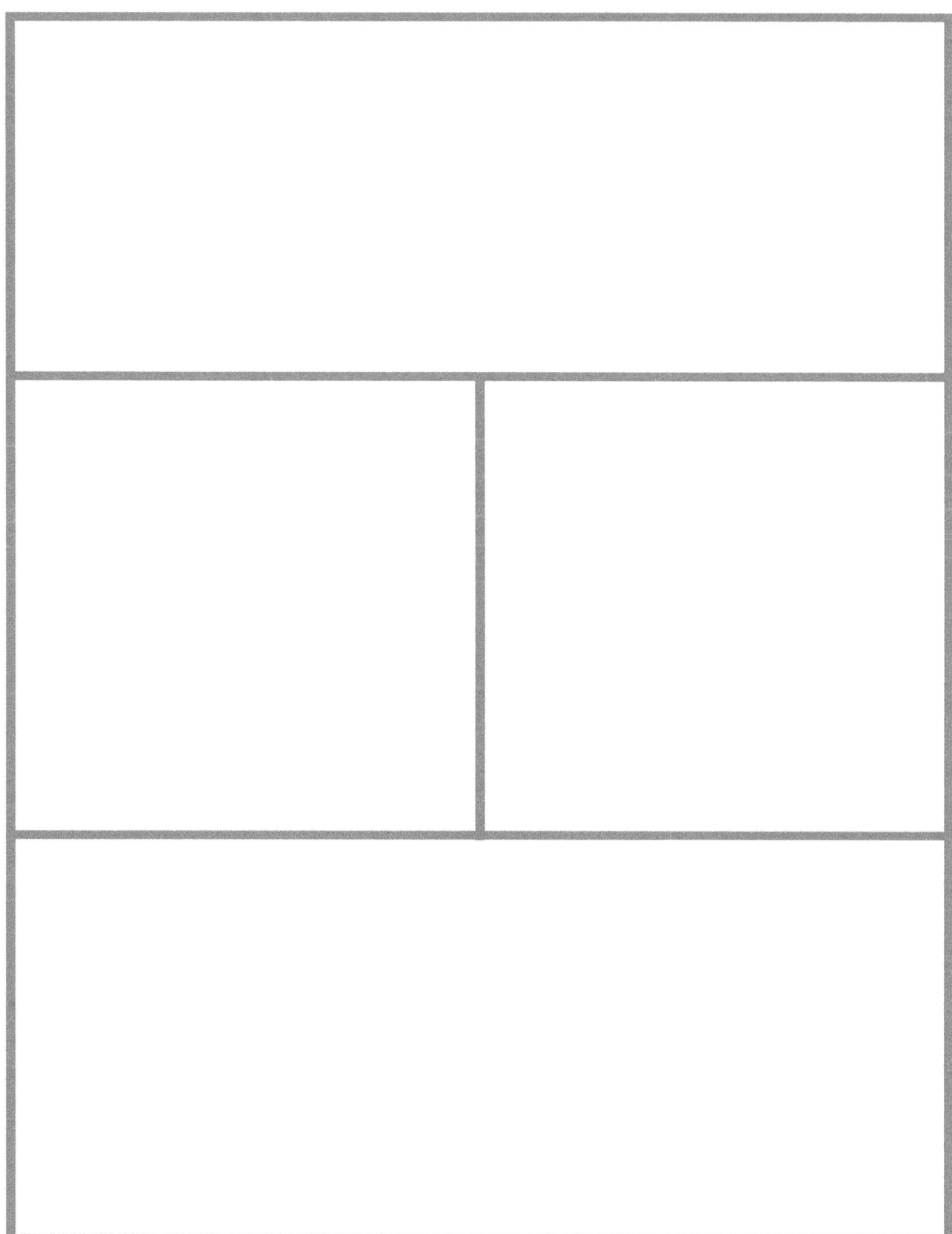

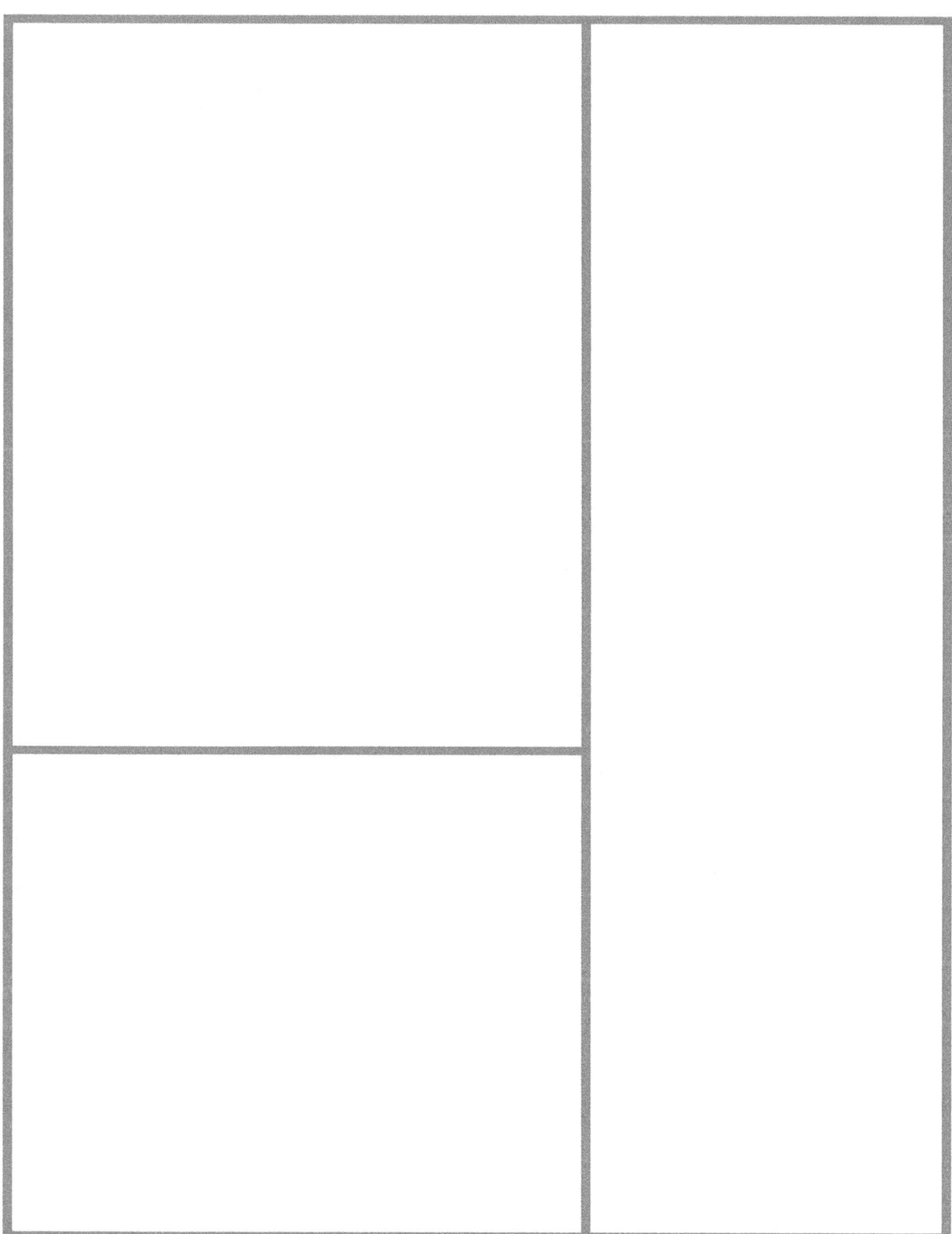

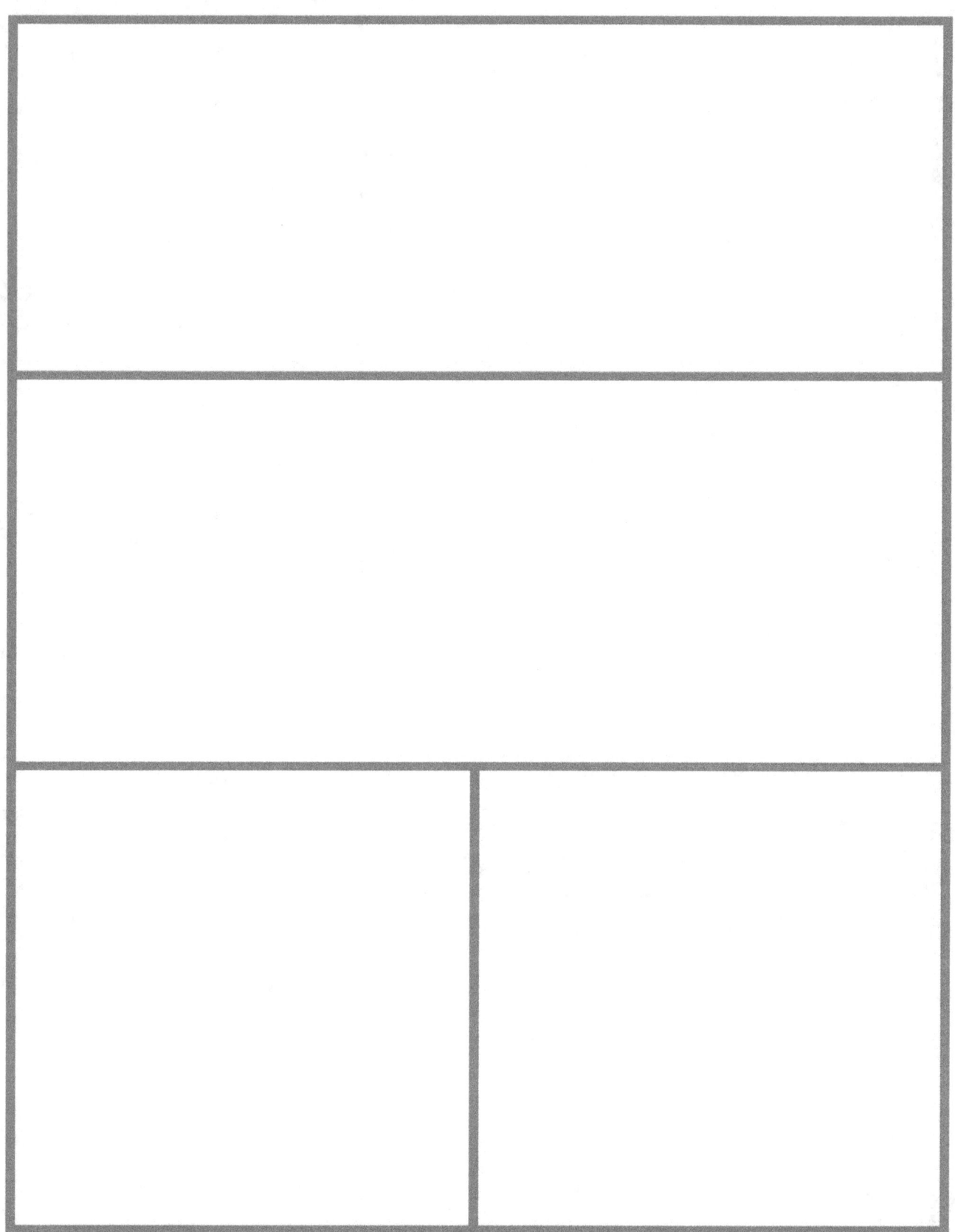

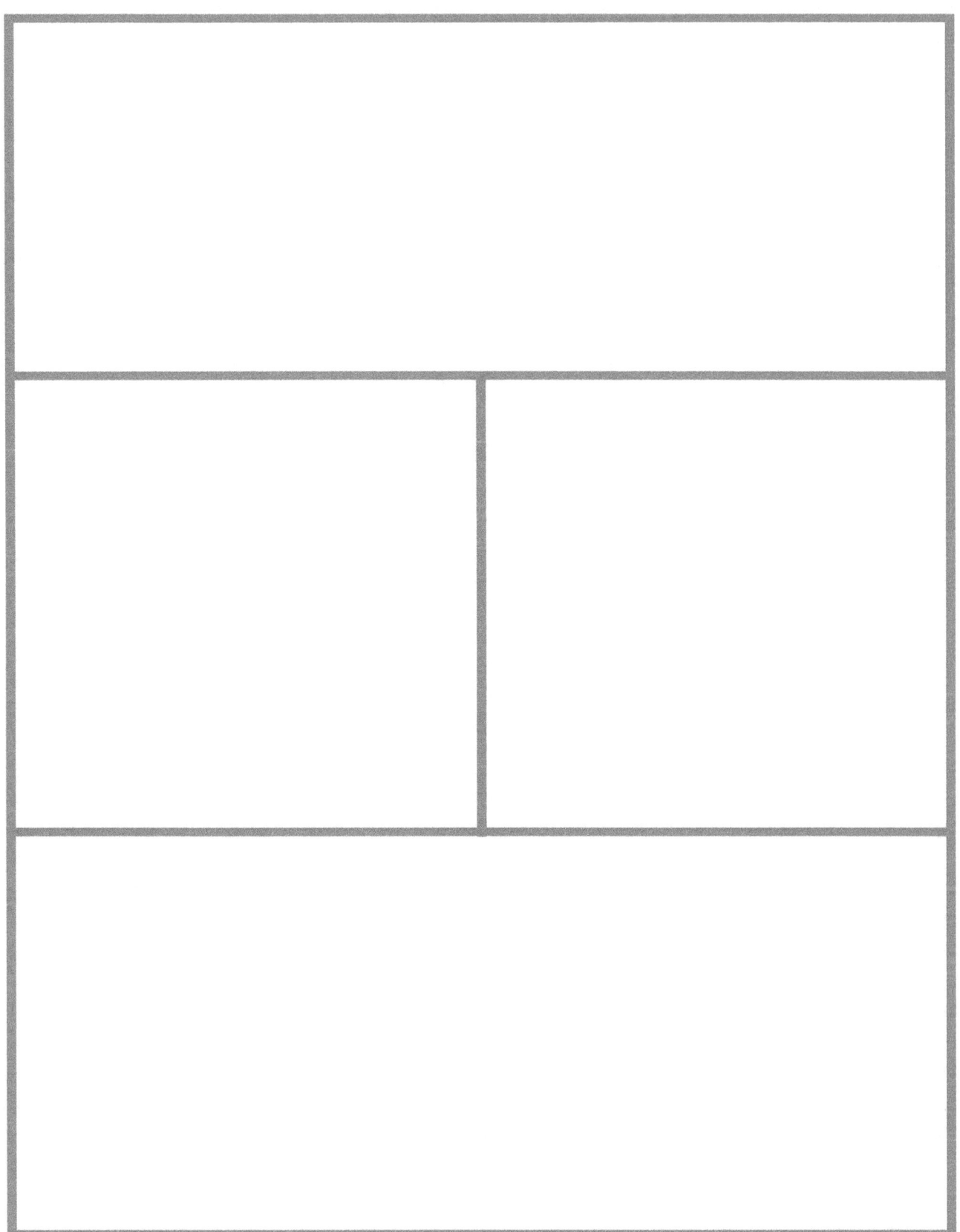

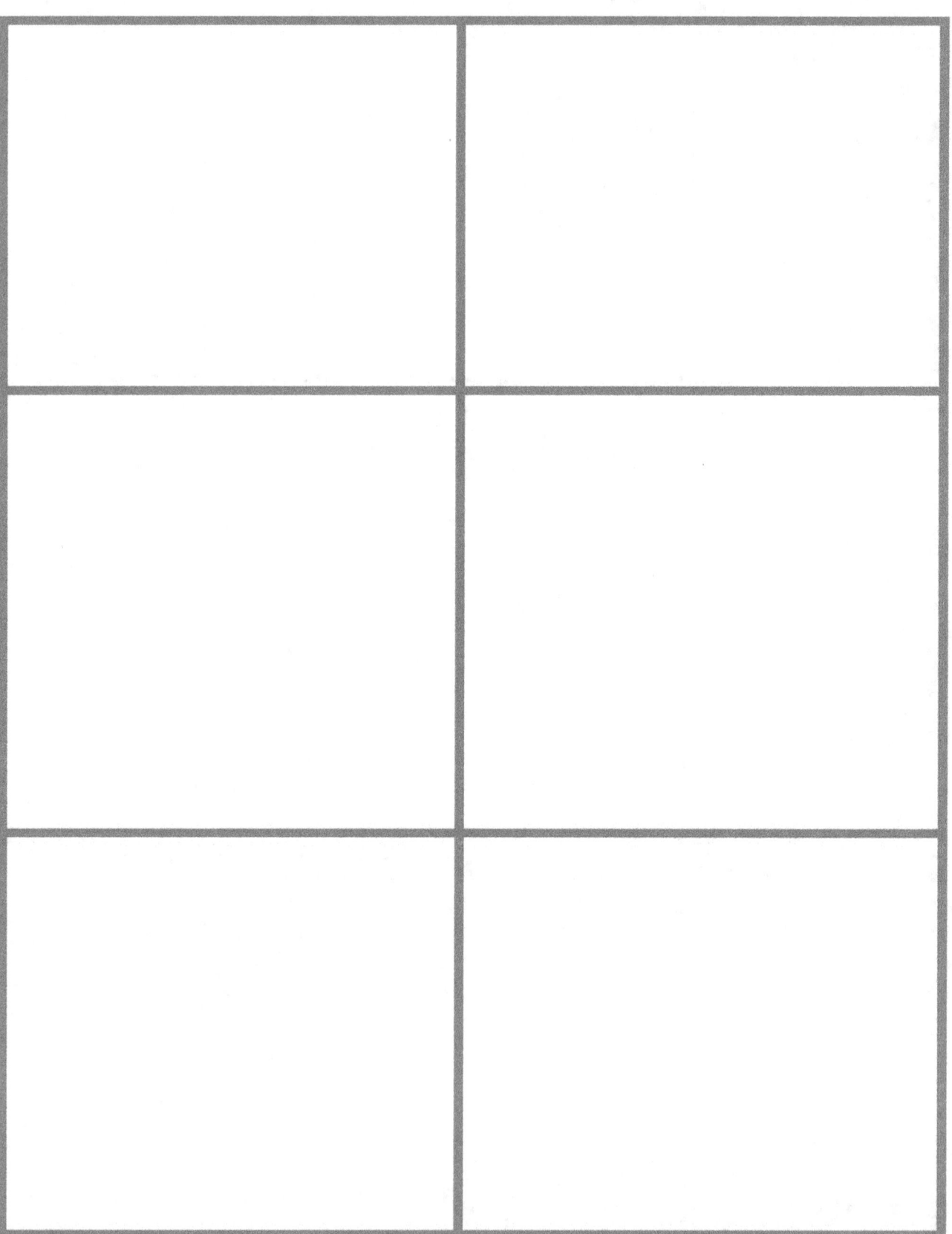

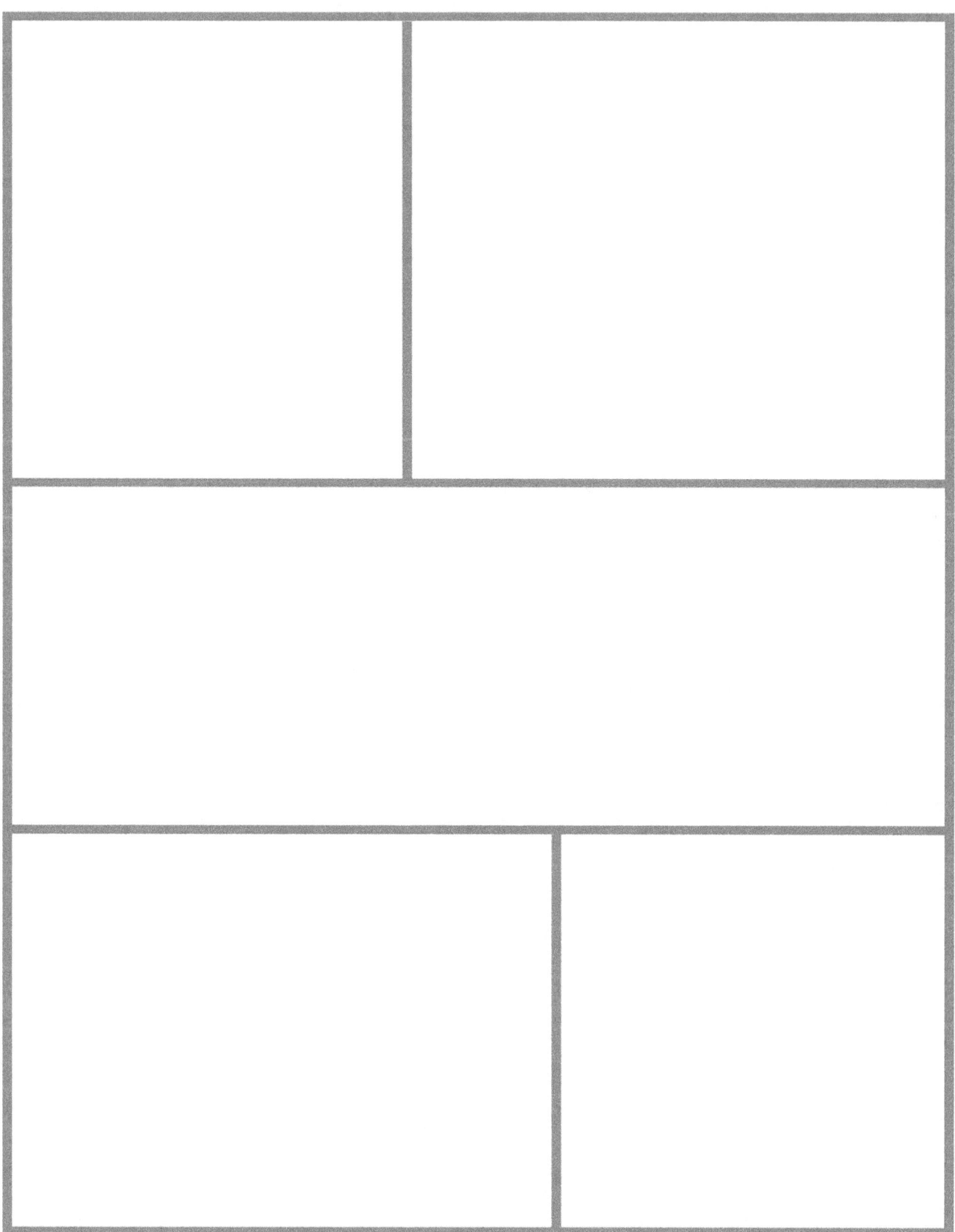

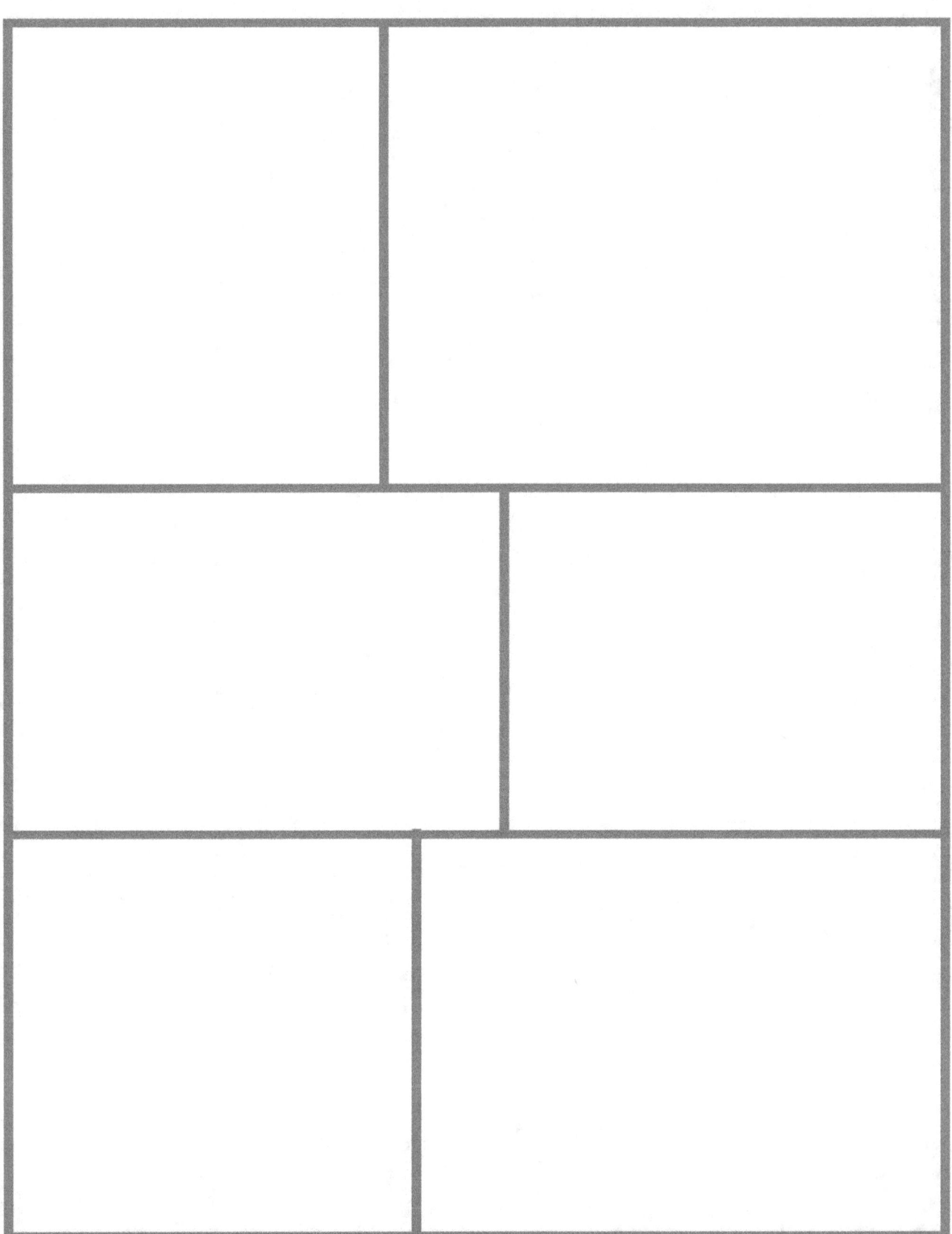

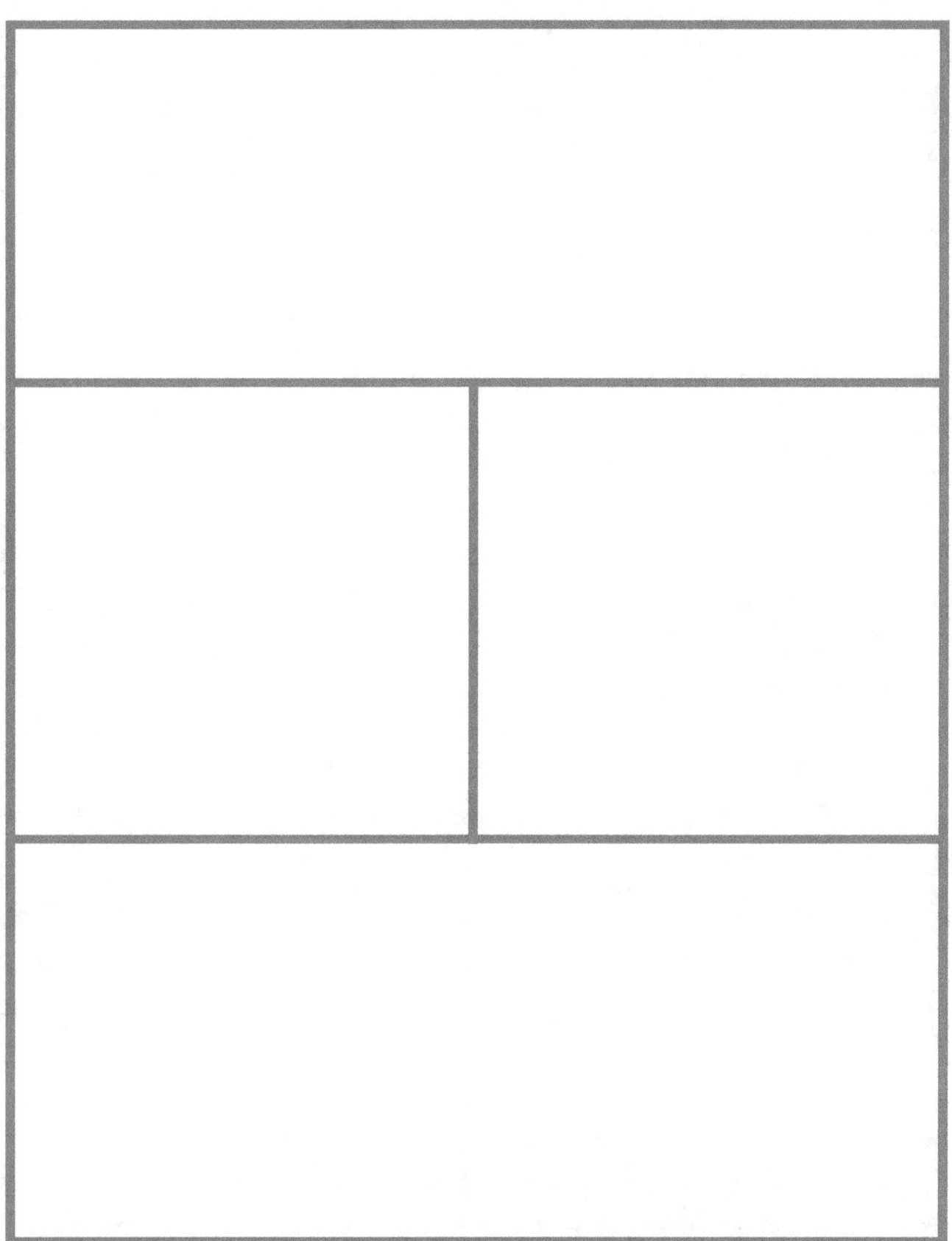

EDUCATION IS THE KEY TO HAPPINESS

www.MikazukiPublishingHouse.com

If you are an author and are interested in working with a traditional publisher, then submit your manuscripts or works to:

authors@MikazukiPublishingHouse.com